Integrity's

Impact

To Dave Nachman:
Metrics, metrics, metrics. Where's
the time to make money? :)

10 JUN 06

another
example
of

UNCOMMON
TECHNOLOGY

Integrity's Impact

Your Practical Guide To Integrity's Power, Benefits, & Use

Mark A. Willson

Book One of the

CROSSFIRE METHOD

The New, Practical, and Straightforward Approach
to Solving 21st Century Business Problems

Troubleshooter's Arsenal 1: Integrity's Impact
by Mark A. Willson

Book one of the CrossFire Method.

First Edition: First Printing [A]

Published by Uncommon Technology Incorporated
5400 Carillon Point, Kirkland WA 98033 USA
Telephone: 800.910.9000 *Fax:* 800.910.9505
Web: www.UncommonTechnology.com
Email: Publishing@UncommonTechnology.com

Quantity Purchases: Uncommon Technology publications can be purchased at a substantial discount for educational, business, promotional, or charitable use. Please contact us for more details.

Trade and Service Marks: *Uncommon Technology, UTI,* the UTI starburst logo, *CrossFire Method, Troubleshooter's* series designations, *Troubleshooter's Arsenal, Integrity's Impact,* "Where reality is only a dream away," and related trade dress are trade and/or service marks of Uncommon Technology Incorporated. All other trade and/or service marks are the property of their respective owners.

Disclaimer: While every reasonable precaution has been taken in preparing this book, the publisher and author assume no responsibility for errors or omissions, or from any damages resulting from the use of the information contained herein.

Publisher's Cataloging-in-Publication Data

Willson, Mark A.
   Integrity's impact : your practical guide to integrity's power, benefits, & use / Mark A. Willson. — 1st ed.

      p. ; cm. — (Troubleshooter's arsenal ; one) — (CrossFire method ; book one)
   Includes index.
   ISBN+10: 0-9749658-3-9
   ISBN+13: 978-0-9749658-3-3

1. Business ethics. 2. Leadership—Moral and ethical aspects. I. Title. II. Series: Troubleshooter's arsenal ; one.

HF5387 .W55 2004
174/.4   2004104855

To my parents

Gary and Martha-Mary Willson

*Proving every day that integrity and faith
are a very powerful combination*

Contents

Contents

Contents

Contents

Contents

♦

Preview

Looking beyond the horizon
Imagining the possibilities
Making your own best destiny

Preface

Unexpected Edge

*"Success usually comes to those who are
too busy to be looking for it."*

—Henry Thoreau

I MAGINE yourself alone, sitting on an old log,
deep in a forest. It's a bright, sunny day. Birds
are singing. You're absolutely safe, warm, and
happy. Not a care in the world. Beauty surrounds
you.

Special Delivery

You start to notice a glint in the air in front of you. It's as though some stray rays of sun are reflecting off a bright piece of chrome. As you watch, the glint grows. It takes on more and more substance. Soon a simple, but unusual telescope appears. On its side is a small polished plaque.

Futurescope

See your secret desires fulfilled. To use:

- *Think of something you desire.*

- *Look through the eyepiece.*

- *See your desired future and any obstacles that stand in your way.*

- *When you're finished, the telescope will vanish and you'll be left facing in the direction of your goal.*

- *Whenever you're alone and ready to concentrate, the telescope will automatically reappear as needed.*

Note:

- *The telescope only shows you what's possible. You've got to make it happen.*

- *The more carefully you focus, the clearer things will become.*

- *Use this telescope often to check your progress and to avoid getting lost.*

Future Deliverance

Wow! What would you like to see through that telescope? Think about it. You could observe any possible future, however unlikely. You'd see just how close or far you are from achieving it.

Learn how difficult the journey might be and the obstacles you'd face. Understand what it would be like if you're successful. Such a device would be better than a crystal ball!

Even if you only achieved the tiniest portion of your secret desires, think about how much your life would change. Imagine your success. The money you'd make. The happiness that would be yours. The mistakes and pain you'd avoid. The time and effort you'd save.

I don't know about you, but I'm sold. Where can I order one?

No Need to Wait

Why wait? Get one now. This book contains everything you need to build your very own special telescope from your own personal integrity.

With it you'll free yourself from distractions,
develop intense focus, find more time in your day,
help others to help you, overcome objections, and
neutralize obstacles. As a bonus, you'll even be
able to detect and resolve leadership crises before
they get out of control.

With such a tool, achieving your dreams is
closer than you ever thought possible. Don't delay
your future one more minute.

Act now! Read on. ♦

Preview

Integrity's impact
Sources of integrity's problems
Social and technological change
Components of better integrity
Piecing it together

Online Supplement

www.IntegritysImpact.com/Basics

Chapter 1

Integrity Redefined

"Opportunity is missed by most people because it comes dressed in overalls and looks like work."

—Thomas Edison

OVER the last several years there have been a number of high profile scandals. In business there was Enron, Tyco, and Global Crossing. Political ones include the impeachment of President Clinton, the Bush-Gore vote tally, and the U.N.'s oil-for-food program. Elsewhere was Martha Stewart's obstruction, CBS's *60 Minutes* forged documents, the 9/11 terrorist attack, and far too many others to list.

Integrity's Impact

In all of these situations the actions of certain key individuals ballooned smaller, less significant errors in judgement into monumental disasters of national and even international scope. If those involved had practiced sound personal integrity, no matter how difficult that might've been, the ensuing pain, damage, and outrage would have never reached such overwhelming levels.

|| **CrossFire Guideline #1** ||

When you make a mistake, take immediate responsibility for it. Every moment you delay only makes it grow larger.

These kinds of failures in personal integrity aren't new. They've been around as long as mankind itself. If you look back at almost any period in recent or ancient history, you'll find plenty of examples. Matter of fact, after wars and new discoveries it's probably *the* most frequently documented event.

Our society isn't grossly weaker or stronger than others in this regard. Sometimes it doesn't seem that way though. The strength of the free press in this country makes sure that more of these kinds of problems are reported in the

United States than elsewhere. But then again, more of everything (good and bad) is reported here than anywhere else on the planet.

So if society isn't at fault, then what is? To begin the process of understanding, we need to rephrase that question by changing the "what is?" to "who is?"

CrossFire Guideline #2

Personal integrity is society's first line of defense against disaster.

Headwaters

Technology tends to move very quickly. Unfortunately society and individual attitudes don't move nearly as fast. This difference in speed has people finding themselves increasing isolated from one another. They're experiencing less and less face-to-face human interaction. This can be very difficult to take.

Add into the mix that humans, like most creatures, are naturally lazy. Both honor and integrity require real and constant effort. As the effects of a new technology spreads, the greater the temptation will become for people to act with less and less honor and integrity.

Virtually any new technology or social convention can set off the effect. Especially ones where there hasn't been enough time for widely accept norms of reasonable behavior to be established. These frequently become hotbeds for unreasonable behavior.

CrossFire Guideline #3

New technology not only has to be evaluated for its usefulness, but for the way it effects people. Sometimes you'll find those costs are way too high.

Socio-Tech

The Internet is an excellent example of one such breeding ground. In this realm it's very easy to be totally anonymous. Certain specific aspects of the Internet makes this especially easy:

• Information moves from one place to another moment-by-moment in nearly an unlimited number of ways.

• A huge number of corporate and personal firewalls exist to protect their networks and their systems from hackers by placing a shroud of secrecy over their user's activity.

• A system can be connected anywhere on the Internet and still have full access.

Combined, these technological features have inadvertently created the perfect medium for deception. Anyone who wants to hide in the shadows will feel right at home here. Due to the ease of anonymity, crimes and issues that were rare or nonexistent just a few years ago have reached epidemic proportions. Identity theft, spam, predatory pedophiles, credit card fraud, porn, and even terrorist activities are all examples of this new crime wave.

This kind of breakdown is what can happen anytime that:

• personal self-control is too weak.

• the opportunities for poor behavior are too plentiful.

• the potential gains are too high.

• the risks of being caught are too small.

CrossFire Guideline #4

Newer social conventions and technologies are often abused by those with poor or faulty personal integrity.

The Internet isn't alone with its problems. Any recently developed social situation or technology, especially those involving communications, is a potential target. Examples include cell phones, PDAs, plus even relatively low technology devices like fax machines, beepers, cameras, and others.

So what? Does this mean that as a species we're all descending into chaos? Nope. For most people on this planet, the quality of life gets better with each passing year. But it's also a fact that there will always be those that will take advantage of others when given half a chance.

What's needed is an easy way for everyone to truly understand integrity and what they can do to improve their own. This way people can avoid becoming part of the problem and instead, become part of the solution.

CrossFire Guideline #5

Understanding your own state of integrity is the first step toward creating a better future for everyone.

Facets of Practical Integrity

The concept of integrity isn't very clear in most people's minds. For them its definition is a confused jumble of generalizations gathered from a wide variety of vague sources in their younger years. Overall it seems anchored more on theory than reality. To really understand and achieve practical integrity, we need to redefine the term itself.

Honor

Simple integrity can be useful, but by itself it's not nearly enough. The greatest tyrant in the world can be evil to an extreme and still have high integrity. The word integrity just means that you're consistent in your behavior. All your actions flow from a stable and unchanging set of beliefs or rules. By definition, virtually any machine has high integrity.

CrossFire Guideline #6

Integrity without honor is only useful to tyrants and machines.

Honor transforms simple integrity into something of beauty. Its addition helps you act in a way that brings credit to you and those around you. Only with this extension, does the concept of integrity start to take on the classical meaning that most of us expect.

Focus

Even with honor added in, integrity is still just a theory. To change that, we need to mix in two other misunderstood concepts—focus and leadership. Integrity can't exist in the real world without both of them.

If integrity is the set of personal rules that you've decided to live by, then focus controls how you actually use them in your daily life.

Focus is more than just the ability to evaluate a set of rules to make decisions. It's the basic understanding of where you want to go in life and how you expect to get there. With it you prioritize the tasks ahead of you and make conscious decisions about how best to spend your time and resources in order to accomplish them.

CrossFire Guideline #7

*Integrity may decide what's right,
but focus makes it meaningful.*

Its more subtle purpose is to eliminate or minimize the number of mistakes you make along the way. It also has the added benefit of conserving your time and resources for those activities that are really important to your goals.

Leadership

The second misunderstood ingredient is leadership. This facet of integrity adds in the commonly understood ability to communicate clearly and motivate others. What isn't so clear is the less obvious transfer of rules, decisions, and priorities in such a way that those following your directions can easily understand them. To be successful this will require even greater focus on your part.

	CrossFire Guideline #8	
	Practical integrity	
	requires leadership	
	of a more refined nature.	

Putting the Pieces Together

You can't help but be a person of outstanding integrity if you:

√ have sound rules to live by (integrity).

√ consistently and conscientiously use those rules to help you make the right decisions (focus).

√ bring positive credit to yourself and those around you (honor).

√ help others to see the right path (leadership).

In broad strokes, this book was written to help you become that honorable person.

To be more. To expect more. To achieve more. Right now! ♦

Preview

Defining you

Lighting up your path

Playing your cards face up

Keeping promises and secrets

Dealing with fear

Knowing what's right

Drifters

Blame game

The power of the package

Online Supplement

www.IntegritysImpact.com/Ethics

Troubleshooter's Arsenal 1

Chapter **2**

Stainless Steel You

"If you can't get rid of the skeleton in your closet, you'd best teach it to dance."

—George Bernard Shaw

W HO are you? Every day since you were born, you've been unconsciously working to answer that question. Answering it with your actions. Actions define who you are. What you think and what you dream doesn't matter if you never translate them into action.

|| **CrossFire Guideline #9**
Your actions, not your thinking, defines who you really are. ||

Walking on Stage

Most of us have similar stories about how we got to be who we are. Most likely, when you were a young child your parents, siblings, and friends defined your understanding of the world around you and where you fit in. You tested your limits in basic ways and had a good grasp of the words "yes" and "no"—especially "no."

As a teenager, more information started to come in. School, television, books, and other sources, plus your growing number of acquaintances gave you a sense of community and where you stood in it.

As opportunities to make your own choices without supervision increased, you succeeded and failed in larger and larger ways. You were testing society's and your own personal limits. Going after the things you thought you wanted, whether they really made sense or not, became your primary activity. Your basic understanding of yourself took on a more solid shape.

But as adults, most of us haven't progressed very far from that teenage view of ourselves. We still tend to rely on its incomplete and immature definition of who we are. Life, career, family, and our own inattention frequently distract us from getting around to improving it.

Like an unfinished oil painting, it becomes harder and harder to change significantly as time passes. Don't leave it incomplete. Instead take the time to turn it into something beautiful. Your masterpiece.

CrossFire Guideline #10

The longer you wait fix anything, the more difficult it becomes.

How you act in difficult situations has a dramatic effect on the odds of your success. To help you along, let's take a look at how you can adjust some of your personal rules of conduct. Even small changes can have a huge positive impact on you and your performance. The idea is to get you thinking about who you are versus the person you really want to be.

You're worth the effort, right?

CrossFire Guideline #11

Most people watch. Heros act.
Be a hero everyday.

Let There Be Light

Feelings of obligation, laziness, hesitation, peer pressure, social pressure, money (or the lack of), loneliness, and wanting to be liked/loved are just a few of the reasons that we waste so much of our day. Most of these issues revolve around not having a clear understanding of what we want and what we're willing to do to get it.

Successfully employing the following guidelines will help you when all else fails. They're your last line of defense. Think of them as your own personal armor. With the right care, using and developing these important personality characteristics will make many of your problems simply vanish or bounce off harmlessly. Those that remain can be dealt with at your leisure.

CrossFire Guideline #12

*Whatever you do to achieve a goal
will temper it.
Employ the wrong values
and success will turn out
worse than failure.*

Like building muscle, moral fiber strengthens with regular exercise. Use it. Expand it. When you make a mistake and screw up, admit your error and move on. This is your personal key to internal beauty and finding the harmony within yourself and the world around you. (Don't worry. That's the first and last Zen-like statement in this book.)

The world can be a very forbidding place—full of dark rooms, blind alleys, and seedy characters. A little light can change things a lot. Each of the following methods will throw some light on every situation from its own unique angle. If you can turn them all on full, the darkness will disappear.

Searching for an Honest Man

The first and probably hardest piece of personal armor to put on and keep polished is honesty. CrossFire is about doing things in the best way possible. Being honest *is* the best way. Not the easiest, but the best.

Telling lies, leading people on, or suppressing the truth takes a lot of work. To be consistent, you'll need to remember every falsehood you ever tell and then make up even more lies just to keep from being found out. Either that or you'll never again have a long-term relationship with another human being. Lying isn't worth the effort.

If that's not enough, something else is attached to honesty's shirttails: your credibility. Lose it and no one is going to listen to anything that you have to say.

Climbing Out

The hardest part about honesty is getting into the habit. That's why it's so easy for very young children to be so brutally honest. They have little history and have yet to develop any bad habits.

The rest of us have spent so many years avoiding confrontation, embarrassment, or living up to past falsehoods that we've dug ourselves into some pretty deep holes. To get yourself out, start small. Refuse to perpetuate old lies. This can often be embarrassing. Sometimes it's even painful. However, if the lie's old enough and you're lucky, it may just die from a lack of lip service (yours).

CrossFire Guideline #13

Lies take on a life
of their very own.
Then they'll take over yours.
Destroy them
before they destroy you.

Other lies are much harder to kill. Taken credit for other people's work? Apologize and figure out some way to make it up to them (maybe by letting them take credit for something you did).

Lied on a resume? Either come clean with your employer or start looking for another job—telling the truth this time.

Friendly Fire

I haven't held many traditional jobs in my life. Mostly I've worked for my own companies. But in one particular case, I was convinced to take a regular job with a client instead of working on my usual contract basis. After dangling a very large carrot in front of me while the client pushed quite hard from behind, I reluctantly agreed to the arrangement.

After a couple of months on the job, I was in the office of my boss having a casual conversation about the different people that worked for us. He then said, "Us college graduates have got to stick together."

I was stunned. I didn't have a college degree. What was he talking about? After a moment I asked, "What do you mean?"

"Well, other than the two of us, I don't think anyone else that works for us has a degree," he said.

Mumbling something about needing to take care of urgent business that I'd just remembered, I tore out of the room. Gag! Now what was I going to do? Sure I had about three plus years of college, but there wasn't any fancy piece of paper around with a set of initials and my name on it.

I went home early that night to consider my options. Looking over the resume that I had used, the education line showed U.C. Berkeley with EECS next to it. He must have assumed that it was a degree. I meant it to show my major (Electrical Engineering and Computer Science). No matter whose error it was, this was a disaster.

After a sleepless night wrestling with my conscience (I really needed that job at the time), I finally accepted the only possible decision. The obvious one.

The next day, I returned to the office with a copy of my resume in hand. Things were pretty busy, so I didn't get a chance to drop in on my boss until late in the afternoon.

After exchanging pleasantries, I asked him if he remembered his comment regarding our degrees.

"Sure," he smiled.

Swallowing really hard, I continued. "I'm afraid that there's been a misunderstanding," pausing for another big gulp of air. "I don't have a degree."

Startled, he looked at me as though I was some bugeyed alien asking for directions to the White House. I handed him my resume with the education line circled, and pointed. "See that's my major, not my degree."

Silence. More silence. Worried that his higher brain functions may have seized, I decided to offer him an easy exit. With a forced smile, I said, "Guess I'm out of a job, huh?"

That *got his attention. He answered, "Hmm."*

Uh oh, I thought to myself, I'm dead.

A few more moments of silence passed. He starred blankly. Then he started asking questions. Questions about my education, resumes, and background. Eventually, he was satisfied that I was still valuable and decided not to have me escorted out the door.

Playing Russian Roulette with one's career is gut wrenching at the least and fatal at worst. I recommend avoiding it at all costs.

The longer you've lived, the harder it is to repair the damage. However, it's worth the effort. People will notice the difference, however subtle it may seem to you. As an additional bonus, your life will get easier with every step you take.

Remember, no one's perfect. Learn from your mistakes. Try harder.

One last point. Don't do something unforgivable in honesty's name. If your actions will hurt others, just to help you or make you feel better, then keep your mouth shut.

Otherwise, being honest can be a bit boring. No one likes that. Instead we all want to be seen as exciting, intelligent, funny, and interesting. If you're like me, you enjoy telling stories. Nothing wrong with that. Just draw a clear line between fact and fiction. Respect is what you'll gain.

Honorable Mention

I'm talking about keeping your word. Promises. Secrets. This is where honesty takes on a more tangible form. To be truly honorable your word must be your bond, your contract.

When you say that you're not going to repeat what someone is about to tell you (like in an interview), you better keep quiet. If you don't, the only surprise you'll have is if anyone ever takes you into their confidence again.

An Affair to Forget

A difficult, but not uncommon, personal situation that you might find yourself in is that a friend of yours is having an affair. His wife doesn't know. Should you tell her?

Probably not. Just a few of the reasons are:

- *She may already know and by "informing" her, you'll end up publicly humiliating her (even if it's just you as the public).*

- *Both of them may hold you responsible for any breakup, due to your involvement. You may end up never seeing your friend or the wife again.*

- *You're not the morality police.*

- *No matter what things look like, you could be wrong.*

However, you should avoid lying or covering up for him. If asked directly by his wife, answer with silence or "this is a matter for you and your spouse, not me" and walk away.

Telling them what you believe to be the truth, even if they're already sure of the facts, won't help anyone. This is a problem that the two of them need to work out—it's their relationship after all. The same reasoning still holds even if your friend is the one being cheated on.

Being realistic though, the above situation is almost impossible to get out of. Emotions will quickly escalate and may get totally out of control. So the previous advice may not work. If it doesn't, just try to say the minimum necessary to extract yourself safely from the confrontation. When the opening comes, leave. Don't make the mistake of hesitating. It never gets any better, only worse.

Finding yourself stuck in a swamp of lies and deceit created by somebody else is a lousy place to find yourself. Avoid going there. You'll hate it and, most likely, you'll end up hating the person who put you there.

All things have their limits, and promises and secrets are no exception. You're not a doctor or a lawyer (unless you are). If you're being asked to suppress information about an illegal, unethical, or harmful act, take prudent action.

If you've got reason to believe that what you've been told is serious and urgent, bring it to the attention of the proper people. As with honesty, make sure that your actions are for the right reasons.

A word of caution. Don't treat your word lightly. Always think twice before committing to a promise or secret.

Promises can be so strong that they'll hold up in court where a written contract might not. Exercise caution in what you agree to. Even if you're not keeping track of what you're saying, somebody else is.

And remember that keeping your word can be *very* expensive. Often in more ways than one. The only thing more expensive is *not* keeping it.

CrossFire Guideline #14

*The cost of keeping your word
can be very expensive,
but the cost of not keeping it
is astronomical.*

Braving the Rapids

Starting off on any important endeavor can be daunting. It takes courage with a dash of daring thrown in. If you're too afraid to act, your project will be dead before it's even started. You'll need confidence in your skills and experience to be successful. Using CrossFire allows you to leverage off of someone else's experience. Take advantage of it.

Bravery can pay off in many areas. When researching a problem, interviewing coworkers may become necessary. Some people find doing this is very intimidating, especially their first few times. Not only will you be face-to-face and alone with wide variety of people, you could find yourself talking to some of the top management in the company.

Asking questions like: "What made you think that?" "Why did you do that?" and "Wouldn't it have been better to . . .?" can be difficult to say. At the same time you may be thinking that everyone you're talking with is evaluating your performance and whether you know what you're doing. You could be right about being judged. Regardless, you'll still need to ask the questions. If you don't, you'll never get to the truth and the project will be poorer because of it.

Speak Up

Maybe you find public speaking daunting. You're not alone. Most speakers are nervous before they start talking. It's normal. It'll be okay. You'll survive.

When using CrossFire, the end of each project stage is accompanied by a presentation to the Project Team. If you're leading the project, that means you.

At that point the other members of the team shouldn't be strangers, but you might still find it intimidating. Don't let it be. This is where being optimistic can really help. Have faith in CrossFire and your convictions. When you find yourself in front of the group, you'll know more about the situation than anyone else in the room.

Check your fear at the door and you'll find it really easy to shine.

|| **CrossFire Guideline #15**

Don't let life's scary parts stop you from reaching for your dreams. ||

Ethics Isn't Ethnic

Ethics can be a sticky issue. Like a giant piece of fly paper, it covers the unethical shortcuts to our desires. At times finding a clear path to your goals isn't an easy task. The bigger the desire and the more difficult it is to obtain, the more tempting the wrong path will become. Resist any urges that you may have. If you act unethically, you'll lose the battle before you've even begun.

CrossFire Guideline #16

Playing fair isn't a limitation.
It's freedom.

When in doubt, test your motives. Imagine that somehow, someway a clear, detailed, and unbiased report of your actions is unexpectedly published on the front page of the *New York Times*. Also assume that everyone you've ever known or will ever meet in your life actually reads and remembers that article. If that leaves you feeling worried, uneasy, or even slightly shameful, it's unethical. (Having others read about you and your partner's sexual relationship would probably be embarrassing, but not shameful.)

For this check to work though, you must use it *before* you act. Your mind's a funny thing. It must justify every single action you take. If it doesn't, you'll literally go crazy. Once you've done something unethical, your mind *will* find a way to justify your actions—regardless of how faulty that reasoning may be. This is why the great majority

2: Stainless Steel You

of people in prison are always innocent in their own eyes.

Unethical behavior lives in the shadows. Comfort comes from the darkness, from not being seen. The reasoning behind your actions is immaterial. Cheating, spying, using insider information, pretending to be someone else, harming or letting someone be harmed, and giving false testimony are just a few examples of where ethical standards are more important than the legal ones.

CrossFire Guideline #17

Always try hard to do what's right.
It pays very well—little guilt
and fewer worries for life.

The Dangerous Gift

Let's say that you and a colleague are competing for the same department manager's position. You also happen to be aware of a small unreported gift (large enough it should have been reported, small enough to be unimportant) that the other person received from a vendor after they were awarded a lucrative contract. Should you report the gift to management?

Nope. A few reasons not to are:

- *It will be seen (correctly or not) as an attempt by you to get ahead by stepping on someone else.*

- *You're not the enforcer of the employee's handbook (unless you are).*

- *They may have already given the gift harmlessly away.*

- *When your colleague and others find out, they'll be out for your blood (maybe literally).*

- *No matter what it looks like, you could be wrong.*

If you're truly concerned, approach your colleague casually and ask about the gift. Tread softly. Make very sure that he understands that you're really concerned about this matter and you're not out to trap or torpedo him. Mean it! Otherwise, stay quiet.

(On the other side of the coin, what would you do if you found yourself in the other guy's spot? Hopefully, you wouldn't hang onto the gift. If you did, you'd needlessly endanger your job, career, and reputation. All for a stupid, insignificant trinket.)

It's these kinds of situations where the rich and famous frequently trip and fall flat on their face. Tiny, nearly worthless transgressions. Most of the time it's because they've lost either their perspective or they believe they don't have to follow the same rules that everybody else does. Don't set yourself up for the same fall.

But not all temptations are insignificant. The bigger and more important the situation, the larger the payoff can be to short-circuit society's and your own personal code of conduct. Regardless of the amount, you've got to find the will to resist.

It's an ironic fact of life that the most likely time to be faced with a large ethical dilemma is at the exact moment that you're at your weakest. All that I can suggest is that if you make the right choice, you'll probably look back on it as one of the proudest moments in your life. Don't throw that memory away.

All of us have our own moral compass to help us on life's journey. Use it. Elevate your standards. Pretend that you're always in the spotlight.

Do this and you'll be ready to bask in the limelight, instead of panic, if the public eye should ever turn its icy glare toward you.

Defusing the Pretty Bomb

Many times the difference between acting in an ethical manner and not is simply asking the right question. For example, you might approach your company about some old piece of equipment that never gets used anymore versus just taking it.

Fear of being turned down, believing that the ends justify the means, or our own laziness can stop us from acting in an ethical manner. Don't assume it'll be okay. It could be a *big* mistake.

CrossFire Guideline #18

Confirming instead of assuming is often the only difference between ethical and unethical behavior.

Even if you do get away with it, someone will always know—you. Trashing your conscience is not the path to a stress-free life.

Stepping Up to the Plate

Most people just drift through life, letting its random currents dictate their successes and failures. It's hard to blame them for taking the easy route. It's so seductive.

No matter what happens to them, they always have someone to blame when things go badly. A boss. Parents. Childhood. Genes. The government. God. The list is endless. Only one person escapes all blame—themselves. It's depressing.

> ## CrossFire Guideline #19
>
> *Don't blame others for your problems, even when it's true. Nothing, nothing good will ever come of it.*

Instead, really *live* life. No excuses no matter how good they may be. *Eagerly accept full responsibility for all your highs* and *lows.* When you make mistakes, learn from them. This is a much happier and more satisfying way to live your life. I guarantee it.

Much of the stress in our lives comes from dealing with problems. But that's our job. So, quit worrying about it. If your company didn't have problems, why would it need you?

Take full responsibility for your personal and professional life. You'll never regret it.

CrossFire Guideline #20

*Your job, everyone's job,
is to solve problems.
This isn't a burden.
It's job security.*

Stainless Steel Integrity

Integrity sums up the important components of your personal and professional demeanor. Your honesty, honor, bravery, ethics, and responsibility are all tied together in one neat package. How your integrity appears to the outside world depends on your attention to those areas. The strength of your integrity is only as strong as your weakest characteristic.

People may dislike what you represent—whatever that may be. They may dislike you personally for a variety of reasons (or even for no reason at all). But if you jealously maintain and protect your integrity, most will begrudging respect you for your convictions. They'll know that they can work with you when it's required. Don't throw it all away by giving your detractors a reason to drag your good name through the mud.

Looking at it in a different way, integrity is just another word for dependability. Whatever you do will have consistent and predictable results. The risks of being flaky or acting out of character are minimal. Companies like that. They want to see things started and finished with a minimum of fuss and bother. Your integrity is a proud badge for all to see.

CrossFire Guideline #21

When you have high integrity, the people you work with may not like you, but they will respect you.

A person with high integrity is a pleasure to do business with. This isn't to say that you'll necessarily like what they're doing, but they'll be consistent. No nasty surprises. This is extremely important for doing well with CrossFire. After all if you're not dependable, why would anything be that you create?

Suiting Up

Putting your personal armor on will help you in ways that you'd never expect and will rarely see. Each piece has its own way of protecting you from dangerous or ruinous situations. Maintain it well.

With regular attention, which will soon become automatic, it'll stay bright and shiny. Old, rusty armor with lots of holes in it isn't worth the trouble. Protect it. It's your last line of defense.

Many professionals, some very successful, operate without any beliefs in place except making a dollar. When difficult choices appear, they roll the dice and pick a direction. Sometimes they're lucky, sometimes they're not. One thing's for sure. They *will* lose eventually. When they do, their way of making a living may totally disappear. Don't be like them. It's like dancing in a minefield. Stupid.

Your Protection

For a quick recap on what makes up your personal armor, here are the components for easy reference:

√ Be honest and open.

√ Make your word your bond.

√ Act bravely with a dash of daring.

√ Hold yourself to the highest ethical standards.

√ Take full responsibility for all aspects of your personal and professional life.

√ Maintain high personal integrity.

Note that the list doesn't include being smart or quick. Those can be very helpful for making you a better tool in a given circumstance, but they won't protect you from someone or something that's out to get you.

CrossFire Guideline #22

Being smart and fast is helpful,
but won't help you avoid
being stabbed in the back.

On the contrary, sometimes being smart can work against you. It may allow you to distinguish between one large problem and many smaller ones headed your way. (It can be a bit unnerving to see ten different small arrows coming at you, instead of just one big one.)

No one's perfect and we can all use some improvement. Work on it. ♦

Preview

What's holding you back?
Protecting your weaknesses
Showing respect
Distortions
Knowing more than expected
Finding what you need
Going too far
Dialing up the intensity
Independent success
Your new tools

Online Supplement

www.IntegritysImpact.com/Distractions

Chapter **3**

Shields Up!

---

*"Argue for your limitations, and sure
enough they're yours."*

—Richard Bach

L IFE is full of distractions. Thousands and
thousands of them compete for your attention every single day. Many go in below
your radar and work on your subconscious.
Others are right in your face, daring you to ignore
them. Somehow, despite all the clutter, you've got
to find the time and energy necessary to focus on
making your dreams come true.

So, how do you find the freedom to succeed? By cutting all unnecessary, time wasting, and attention diverting activities from your life. I'm not suggesting that you ignore your friends, family, loved ones, or other interests. But if you look carefully, you'll find that much of your precious time and energy isn't spent on those. Instead, it's consumed by other tasks that you're not aware of or don't really care about.

CrossFire Guideline #23

Some people get a lot more done than most by avoiding activities that they don't really care about. Be one of them.

Becoming distracted or wasting time usually isn't deliberate, but it still happens. Time passes whether you use it wisely or not. Many of us end up facing a mid-life crisis when we realize that we've got less life left than is required to do everything that we want to do. Winning requires you to dump the junk and find a good balance for the rest.

This chapter will show you secret and often hidden ways to eliminate these subtle success killers. Even with your very busy life (that's probably constantly getting busier), you'll find that these methods aren't hard. The more you use them, the easier and more effective they become. After a while, using them will become so automatic that you won't even be aware that you're doing it.

Ready to clear the decks?

Today's Specials

In the previous chapter we talked about protecting yourself from problems and distractions through a passive defense. It discussed certain core rules of conduct that make many of these types of issues simply disappear.

In this chapter we're going to examine more active defenses. This collection of shields operates between your personal armor and the immediate outside world. When problems and distractions zero in on you, your shields will take the majority of the blows. They work by adding more protection to your armor's weakest areas.

While armor protects you from all angles, shields usually have to be placed properly to protect you. In the following sections, you'll find several automatic, self-positioning shields. Each will protect a particular vital area that's known to come under frequent attack. You'll find that they're really handy when you're in a tough spot.

Don't forget that not turning them on or leaving them at home exposes you to needless risk. They're transparent, automatic (with practice), weigh nothing, and only require a small amount of maintenance. So why not use them?

Respectable Behavior

The first shield is being courteous. Sounds silly, but it isn't. It's often ignored in the very busy world of business.

Simple courtesy is a tangible way of showing respect for another. When dealing with people, try to worry more about their needs than your own. Make them comfortable, at ease with you and the situation.

CrossFire Guideline #24

*When people are relaxed
and comfortable,
they'll be more open to new ideas
and less likely to be undermining.*

You can accomplish this with simple planning and a dose of graciousness. Remember what your mother taught you and tailor it to the setting and the situation. Some suggestions:

- Try to keep your head near the same level as theirs. If they're standing, offer them a chair. If they're sitting, be brief or ask if you can sit down.

- Hold doors open for people, regardless of their sex.

- Offer someone a drink (nonalcoholic) before starting a meeting if it might take more than thirty minutes.

- Use a pleasant and level voice without slipping into a monotone.

- In meetings take a break, whether you want to or not, about every ninety minutes.

- Let people eat, or better yet feed them, if a meeting goes over three hours.

- If you must criticize someone, do it in private. Get their side of the story first. Help them improve by telling them how to avoid the problem in the future.

- Don't overdress or underdress for the situation (this is harder than it might sound).

- Try to allow someone who commits a blunder a gracious way to extract themselves from their predicament (this is *very* important in certain international situations).

- Be neat, clean, and presentable at all times.

- Let people be part of the process by asking for and using, whenever possible, their opinions and ideas (with due credit).

Caring about the people you work with and their needs is the grease that makes for a smooth flowing operation. When disagreement and conflict appear, your past performance will make progress still possible. Make the effort.

Cutting Across the Bias

Each of us have our own biases. That's only natural. But as a professional, you're expected not to let them affect your judgement or your performance.

A manager criticizes a subordinate in front of others. A coworker damages another's career, just because he can. Vendettas. Pettiness. Ill manners. Bigotry. Sexism. Intolerance of all kinds. None of them have any place in your words or actions.

Ski Bums

Long ago I had an interview for a project at a top overnight express delivery company. It was early winter. The interview was scheduled for a Friday in the late afternoon. This was somewhat unusual. Most people are usually anxious to start the weekend early. Obviously, the manager I was meeting wasn't one of them.

When I got there, he was quite punctual and greeted me in the lobby. His manner was friendly, but subdued. Ushered into his small office, I scanned the walls and desk quickly. I always like to find something about the person I'm interviewing with that I can connect with. He had a number of skiing pictures on the wall. I asked "Looks like you really like skiing."

He nodded his head up and down and pushed an ashtray over to my side of the desk. He asked if I'd like to smoke. I said that I didn't smoke and went back to the skiing. "I'm not much of a skier myself," I admitted. "If I'm lucky, I might get out once a year."

After my comment, his manner totally changed. He beamed and started talking a mile a minute. I had passed a test. What test, I hadn't a clue. After about an hour of talking, he was relaxed enough that I asked him why his attitude had changed early in the interview.

He looked kind of sheepish and said "I have a confession to make. I hate skiers and smokers. Those pictures are of my son. I actually don't have anything against the sport, but I refuse to hire a contractor that's a skier. That's why I had you wait until Friday to interview. Most skiers won't even show up."

Hesitating for a moment, he went on. "Even when I get desperate and hire one, I end up replacing them in short order. They spend huge amounts of time thinking about the snow, planning their next weekend, extending their week-

end, or getting stuck in the snow. They never get the things done that I hired them for."

"As far as smoking goes," he continued, "we run nearly a clean room environment around the computers. Even if people smoke outside (this was before smoking ordinances), I'm concerned about the equipment being affected by the residue on their clothing. Besides, they always seem to be taking a break."

Whether this manager was wrong or right, is unimportant. What is important is that his judgement was substantially affected. Know your biases. Find a way to compensate for the unreasonable ones.

CrossFire Guideline #25

*Don't deliberately
set people up to fail.*

Rusty Knowledge

Much of what you've learned in life is just as accurate today as the day you were taught it. History, mathematics, mechanics, woodworking, sewing, and many more subjects change at a glacial pace. Others like business, technology, information management, medicine, and science advance at a much faster rate.

These fields are constantly growing and evolving. Their pace may vary from year to year, but it never stops. Their unpredictable speed makes what you know today not necessarily useful tomorrow. You need to keep abreast of the rapid changes in business in general as well as in your own field. Read newspapers, books, trade journals, and magazines. Take classes, seminars, workshops, video courses, and other instruction.

Participate in Internet discussion groups, chat rooms, and mailing lists. Talk with people you find interesting. Network and mingle with others at meetings, parties, church, school, family gatherings, and other places.

Avoid isolating yourself at home or work by restricting your communications to electronic form. The more sources of information that you have and the more contacts you make, the better prepared you'll be for life's twists and turns. (This can be extremely valuable if you ever find yourself suddenly out of work.)

Don't limit yourself to your own field. Investigate associated ones and others. Look at general knowledge, politics, fashion, the environment. Expand your hobbies. Get interested in the world at large.

Reality isn't the only source of knowledge either. New ideas are your friends. Stories, fiction, fantasy, art, and music are all places to find creative thinking. Even the classics like Homer,

Plato, Shakespeare, the Bible, and others may fill holes in your understanding that you didn't even know existed.

Think about the awe you felt as a child when you went to your first library. How amazed you were when you found out that they would let you take home whatever books you wanted to read. You probably even tried to checkout an armful of books on your very first visit.

Cruise up and down aisles that you've never been in. Check out things you'd normally never touch. Explore.

You can do the same on the Web. Just follow whatever looks interesting. Forget your boundaries. Let yourself go.

CrossFire Guideline #26

Knowledge is power.
Seek it constantly.
Make it your own.

The power of knowledge isn't just the ability to state facts and statistics. If it were, the ultimate tool for answering the world's problems would be computers and the Internet. Instead, it's the very human skill of taking a mish-mash of divergent ideas, concepts, and information and using them to produce a successful solution to a particular problem.

Organized Isn't a Crime

Dealing with issues and solving problems can be complex. To have any chance of success, you need to stay organized. Organized in your thoughts. Organized in your approach. Organized in your records. Organized in your details. Organized in your presentations. Organized at all times. It can be very hard to do, but it's not impossible.

CrossFire Guideline #27

*Stay organized
regarding your goals.*

If you're using the CrossFire method, most of the organizational work is already done for you. It supplies the structure and framework for you to solve problems quickly. Just follow the method and most of your organizational problems will go away. The only real worry left is the danger of becoming obsessed.

The Possessed

With a potentially overwhelming number of details to keep track of, some people tend to go overboard. They get so wrapped up in staying organized that all forward progress toward their goals comes to a grinding halt. That defeats the whole point of keeping everything straight. Progress becomes slower, instead of faster.

A little chaos, a little messiness can be a good thing.

A Little Dirt Can Help

My hobby is rebuilding old Chrysler musclecars. I also like things neat and tidy. After an evening's work on the cars, I'd always put everything away and make the garage presentable. I was a happy camper, at least for a little while.

After several months I started to get frustrated. Everything looked good, but my progress was like being stuck in molasses. Things were moving, but just barely. It was taking forever to get things done. Something had to change.

I decided to turn down my organizing a couple of notches. I'd only sweep when I was going to be laying down on the floor. If something was a bonafide mess, I'd clean it up right away. Otherwise, I'd ignore it as long as I could stand it.

Infrequently used tools would be put back in the toolbox when I was done with them (so I could find them later). The rest of the tools don't get put away very often, though they all lay around the same general area. Once in a while I'll gather them all up, clean them off, and then put them away. It's sort of my way of hitting the master reset button.

I still get frustrated with the appearance of my garage, but I'm much happier with the rapid progress on the cars. Since that's the true point of the exercise, I can accept the trade-off.

But someday when I'm too old to turn a wrench and they take my driver's license away, I'll go back to having the cleanest garage in town!

As long as you can find what you need, when you or others need it, your organization is good enough. The particular technique you use doesn't really matter.

CrossFire Guideline #28

Be organized only to the point that it saves you time. When in doubt, it's better to be a little less organized than too much.

Just remember that with a project that impacts others, whatever method you use has to be obvious. If you suddenly vanish, someone else has got to be able to pick up the pieces. Piles of notes scattered everywhere isn't particularly helpful to anyone, including you.

Like salt, less is often better for you. Especially for those of us that are perfectionists or tend toward obsessive behavior.

Passion's Fruit

It's very hard to win when you don't believe in the cause. To succeed, you need to feel some passion for what you're doing. Not necessarily a jumping up and down, I can't contain myself level of passion, but at least more than a mild interest. The more demanding the task and the more your brain is required, the more vitally important your passion will become.

Without it, your performance is doomed to mediocrity and your dreams will vaporize. Your lack of interest, above all other causes, can kill any possibility of success. Finding a way for you to feel some passion for what you do is extremely important.

Freckled Believer

A few years after I got out of the Navy, I was working for a small minicomputer manufacturer as its Technical Support Manager.

As part of my job, I'd go out with the sales force on key calls. That way if the prospect had any questions of a technical nature, the salesmen could avoid saying "Um, I don't know" and "I'll have to get back to you on that" over and over again.

(To be fair, at that time most people didn't have a clue as to how a computer worked, much

less a multiuser timesharing one. Even most of the jargon and buzzwords hadn't been invented yet.)

One time in particular I was asked to go out on a call to a small semiconductor equipment manufacturer. There we met with the three principals.

Once the meeting began in earnest, two of them quickly excused themselves and the remaining one, Mike DeSantis, immediately started peppering me with questions. After a moment's hesitation at being caught a little off guard, I fired back answers just as quickly.

Faster and faster the questions came. Soon he started to move away from what was to what could be. Ideas and concepts flew back and forth. The level of intensity was very high. The salesman just watched us in awe.

(I was a little awed myself. I felt like I was taking the oral exam for a couple of years worth of postgraduate Computer Science and Manufacturing.)

However, I knew that particular computer from the individual chip level (no CPU chips in those days) up through the operating system and into the applications. I passionately *believed* that it was capable of much more than anyone ever used it for.

An hour later Mike abruptly ended the conversation. We were quickly ushered out the door. On the drive back to the office, I was very con-

fused about what happened and told the sales-man so.

He told me not to worry about it and thanked me for the help. He ended his comments with "I'm glad it was you and not me defending against that onslaught." He grinned.

Two weeks later he came by my office and told me that we got the order. I was happy, but confused again. I remained that way for some time.

A little less than two years later, I left that job to start my own computer consulting firm. A couple of months after that, I received a tip that a certain semiconductor equipment manufac-turer was looking for some help. I made an appointment to see them.

Until I walked into their offices, I hadn't remembered that I had been there before. Real-izing the connection when Mike greeted me, I smiled broadly.

Once in his office I started off the conversa-tion with "So you decided to buy the computer?"

"Yeah" he answered.

"I've got to ask," hesitating before continuing "what made you finally decide to buy it?"

Thinking for a minute, he answered "I didn't believe anything that the salesman had to say. But you . . ." he said with a serious look on his face. "Anyone who believed in something as much as you did couldn't be totally wrong."

I beamed.

Find the passion. You'll make more money, time will pass more quickly, you'll have a lot more fun, and your genuine interest will be obvious to everyone.

CrossFire Guideline #29

Passion will carry you far higher on the ladder of success than knowledge or endurance alone.

Flight of the Bumblebee

The ability to fine-tune your focus can help you with whatever you work on. Pick some facet of the task that gets you excited about doing your job.

For one person, it might be solving a complex problem. For another, it might be really hating the wasted effort that's taking place and loving the idea of getting rid of it. Maybe the expected technology that may be used is fascinating to you.

Whatever the trigger, leverage off your passions to help rededicate yourself to successfully completing the project. If needed, you can even shift your focus multiple times while on the path to your goals.

Act like a bumblebee working a field and going from flower to flower. Ignore the weeds.

Lawyer's Dilemma

Attorneys new to the field of criminal defense are faced with an interesting problem. How do they focus their efforts so that they're truly effective?

Imagine yourself in their position. If you choose to dedicate your career to protecting the innocent, you'll be poor at defending clients that you know or suspect of being guilty. You'll also run the risk of starving (from constantly losing) and spending most of your life disappointed.

Chasing high fees is an even more hollow goal. It's difficult to translate money into solid performance. After all, it's only a rate of exchange. Even when you convert it into possessions, it rarely feels fulfilling. Pleasing yes, fulfilling no.

If instead you change your goal to putting up the very best defense possible, you can represent the innocent, the guilty, and those with little or no cash. A simple adjustment to your focus would give you a lot more power and success.

With any major task, there are times that you're not going to feel as passionate as you might hope. This is when you rely on your dedication. It's a quiet form of passion. With it you can persevere through the dull or unpleasant parts of your job.

Those tasks that you may not like doing, but understand at a gut level that they need to be done.

CrossFire Guideline #30

*It's not easy to be passionate
about the details of a task.
Focusing on those facets
that you are passionate about
will carry you through the rest.*

With only a little luck, you'll find these dull periods short and infrequent. Push through them. Passion awaits you on the other side.

Declaration of Independence

There are two different types of independence. One is when you're in total control of your goals. Most of the time, this is the freedom you enjoy when chasing your dreams. In business, if you own or run the company, it might be there as well. (Though if you've borrowed money from a bank or have stockholders, they're going to have a say in things.)

Otherwise, you'll report to a person or a group. You can still be independent in your research and assessment. But at some point, you'll need to convince the final decision makers that you're right before you can implement your plans.

After receiving their blessing, you're again free to independently develop and deploy your solution.

Making Your Way Through the Jungle

When working toward your personal goals, you need to understand that only you really care whether or not you achieve them. They're valuable to you and you alone. By definition, this makes you independent of and a bit isolated from those around you.

CrossFire Guideline #31

You're the only person who will ever truly care about your goals.

Having started about a dozen companies, I'm always surprised at the number of naysayers who appear when I try to do something new. People, friends even, will go out of their way to tell me why whatever I want to do is a really bad idea.

There are many reasons why people act this way. *The most common is that your idea might actually be right!* If it turns out that way, it'll mean that they might also be able to succeed if they trusted their instincts. That's a very frightening concept to most people. It's much easier for them just to blow holes through your dreams.

If you've done your homework, know all the facts, and you still believe in your plan, then *ignore what others have to say.* Place your bets and hold on tight. You in for a bumpy ride.

CrossFire Guideline #32

Listen to those whose opinion you respect, but don't let them stop you from doing what you know is right.

Naysayers

There are endless examples of how creative people have succeeded, even with the odds heavily stacked against them. A handful of the classics are:

- *With overwhelming financial, medical, and emotional problems, Charlie Goodyear sought a way to make India rubber practical for automotive tires. Natural rubber melted in heat, cracked when cold, and was adhesive in nature. After five years, he* came up with a nitric acid treatment that solved some of its problems.

Eight more years went by before coming up with the superior vulcanizing process (mixing natural rubber with sulfur and cooking it). Even with patents though, the simplicity of the process made infringement rampant. A great inventor, who was more interested in solving problems than making money, died a very successful but dollar poor man.

• Everyone told Tom Edison that someone else would soon find a practical filament for the electric light bulb. Many people, maybe hundreds, were already searching for it. "Don't even bother looking," they all advised. He ignored them.

In two years he tried more than 1500 basic types of materials. In plants alone he tried over 6000. Even with the huge number of failures, he still beat everyone to a practical solution.

He came up with carbonized cotton thread that lasted 15 hours. Soon he increased it to 40. That was practical. In time and by changing materials, he got it up to 1500 hours (about twice the life of today's average bulb!).

- *In 1965 Fred Smith, future Founder and CEO of Federal Express, wrote an imaginative term paper for Yale University outlining how to efficiently move and reliably deliver time-sensitive packages using a hub and spoke type of arrangement. He got a grade of "C" for his efforts. The professor called it 'an improbable premise.'*

  He put aside the idea for next eight years, while gathering other ideas and additional proof for himself. In the end he proved the student had surpassed his teacher.

Road blocks to your success can also turn up in some startling places. Charles Duell, commissioner of the U.S. Patent Office in 1899, advised Congress and President William McKinley that no more patents needed to be issued.

"The Patent Office should be closed," he wrote. "It's a waste of the taxpayer's money. Everything that can be invented had been invented."

Some people can't see the forest for the trees. Others just can't see anything at all.

For good advice listen to former President Andrew Jackson. He said "Take time to deliberate, but when the time for action arrives, stop thinking and go in."

Don't take forever to make a decision.

Professional Maverick

When you're leading a business project, whether small in size and including only you, or large and involving many, you're *expected* to be independent in your thoughts and actions. Your perspective should be whatever makes the most sense for that organization in that particular situation. Nothing else matters.

> **CrossFire Guideline #33**
>
> *Independence in thought and action will allow you to succeed while others are still sleeping.*

It's unimportant if your views match those of the company, its employees, or others. Make up your own mind based on the facts as you see them.

However, you *do* have to convince your boss or the controlling authority that your approach is the right one. If they don't agree, even after you present your evidence, it's time to reexamine your goals and your approach.

This sounds a lot easier than it is. The individuals involved may be important, powerful, and respected professionals in their fields. Their views can be very intimidating. Resist the temptation to defer to their wisdom just because of their stature. Your experience is just as important as theirs.

The differences between you and them may just be in what you know. However, even intelligent people, in possession of identical information, can legitimately come to radically different conclusions. Your experience will be different from theirs, from mine, from anyone you know.

Trust your feelings until you have reason to change them.

Meeting of One

You need to also keep an eye on yourself. I'm not talking about second guessing your decisions, but in looking at the situation from two different perspectives—a close-in tactical standpoint and a high-flying strategic one. With most of your time spent in the tactical arena, it's easy to forget the real goals of the project.

CrossFire Guideline #34

*The path you pick
to achieve your goals
isn't your primary focus.
Your goals are.*

For that, just ask yourself regularly if what you're doing is in the best interest of the organization. If the answer is ever no, stop and reassess the situation. Figure out what has changed and how to readjust your course before continuing. If you don't meet the strategic aims of the project, the tactical issues won't matter.

An independent view and approach allows you to see what others may miss. Be confident in yourself and your skills.

The Last Mile

How much of an impact a distraction has on you is controlled by how well you know who you really are and exactly where you're going. The clearer those concepts are in your head, the easier you'll find it to ignore distractions.

It's when you're unsure of yourself that you may find yourself spending tremendous amounts of time, even a lifetime, wandering around lost.

CrossFire Guideline #35
Distractions are like gnats.
They can be irritating,
but you'll get a lot more done
if you just ignore them.

This chapter gives you six shields against distractions. They are:

√ Show your respect for others by extending them your courtesy.

√ Understand your own biases and compensate for them reasonably.

√ Ever increase your knowledge and understanding of yourself, your profession, and the world around you.

√ Bring passion to what you do, even when you'd much rather be doing something else.

√ Stay organized so you know what's going on and where to find things, while avoiding obsessing over the details.

√ Stay independent in your thinking and actions to avoid missing opportunities or coming under undue pressure to conform.

Unlike the previous chapter that dealt with your rules of personal conduct, this one focused on easing your efforts. The idea is to make as much of the world around you stay out of your way, if not help you, while you're chasing your dreams.

Even if you're traveling all alone. ♦

Preview

Typing obstacles
People problems
Power parts
Opinion leaders
Weighing the options
Distance's impact
Real issues
Logistical nature
Technical difficulties
Trouble's first name
Calling all issues

Online Supplement

www.IntegritysImpact.com/ObstacleTypes

Chapter 4

Secret Identities

"Obstacles are those frightful things you see when you take your eyes off your goal."

—Henry Ford

YOU can't fight what you don't know about. Understanding obstacles well is required if you want to get really good at neutralizing them. They can be broadly categorized into four distinct types: people, logistics, technical, and communications. Each has its own problems, risks, and priorities.

Since people are usually the biggest obstacles, we'll start off with them.

Restless Natives

As you move toward your goals, some people affected by your project are going to develop concerns about what you're trying to achieve. Even if they never express those doubts out loud, their actions toward you will usually communicate their feeling just as clearly.

While real issues *do* matter, people's nebulous or vague feelings of uneasiness don't necessarily translate into action. Instead, ask more questions. Find out if there really is a problem.

Since people are often illogical, inconsistent, and emotional it's hardly a surprise that they can present such difficult obstacles. Oh well . . . they're human.

> ## CrossFire Guideline #36
>
> *People are the biggest variables*
> *in achieving any goal.*

If handled properly, these difficult obstacles can often be converted into powerful allies. When this happens, the very thing blocking your path is suddenly helping you toward your goals. Quite a transformation and definitely worth shooting for.

Because dealing with people is a very large and diverse topic, books two and three of the *Troubleshooter's Arsenal* series will delve into them in greater detail. For now, we'll just touch on what motivates people and how to assess the size of the obstacle that they present.

Components of Power

Four factors plus one wild card determine the impact of a given individual blocking you from your goals.

These factors, in order of importance, are:

• Stature

• Weight of support

• Proximity

• Legitimacy of concerns

CrossFire Guideline #37

Stature, weight of support, proximity, and legitimacy of concerns determine the size of a human obstacle.

The surprising thing about the above list is that legitimacy (of their concerns) is dead last. If you're like me, you'd expect it to be first. It just goes to show you how pervasive politics are in human relationships.

Because the various factors work as a group, weakness in one or more areas will substantially shrink their overall impact on your project.

Persistence is the wildcard. It multiples the effects of all the others. Even when your opponent has little stature, weight, proximity, or legitimacy, given a high enough level of persistence, you'll eventually have to deal with him.

CrossFire Guideline #38

Persistence can take something small and make it appear big. Sometimes, that's all it takes to win.

Measuring Stature

Stature is the level of respect or deference given by an individual or group to a particular person or group. In corporations, the highest level of stature would usually be held by the CEO or the Board of Directors. In a community, it might be the Mayor or the City Council.

Being political animals by nature, there are virtually endless types and levels of stature attached to each of us. They extend all the way down to a little boy who looks up to his big sister. We confer this respect on others, believing that they're wiser or stronger than us in some way.

Crystal "Ting"

When I was a child, one of the most anxiously awaited events was the extended family gathering. These loud, boisterous, and multifaceted get-togethers always hit a crescendo during the dinner hour.

At the very long table where the adults would sit down to eat (us children relegated to our own tables), two or more conversations were always going at any given moment. If a particularly interesting or contentious topic came up, the conversations would merge as the volume increased.

As the various opinions solidified, the different groups would eventually reach a point where they got stuck, each hammering the other with the same logic over and over.

When the noise level hit the point where jackhammers seem quiet, a sharp "ting" would barely be heard over the din. Then another. Then several. Everyone would stop and look at the source of the sound. The noise level would rapidly drop to zero.

The "ting" was the sound of my great-grandfather, Ed McMahon, lightly striking the side of a paper thin, crystal water goblet with a sterling silver fork.

A thin, but strong man, he never raised his voice. As his intensity increased, his voice would get quieter and quieter. Anyone trying to listen to him would have to strain their ears just to hear him speak.

(Older than the wind, adventurer, motorcyclist before 1900, veteran of the Spanish-American War, husband, Canadian homesteader, father, and eventually retired Postmaster, he got around. He had seen and done more than anyone else we knew.)

Once everyone was quiet, he'd state his considered opinion. Silence would descend on the table while everyone absorbed his comments.

Many times the argument would end right there, and the conversation would move onto a different topic. The only reason that this bunch of smart, independent people often deferred to his judgement was that everyone regarded him as a thoughtful man. He didn't speak just to make his mouth move. His reasoning was sound, fair, and rarely wrong.

From our family's standpoint, he was stature.

When such a person expresses a viewpoint that's in partial or complete opposition to your goals, you've got a big problem. Though they may be commenting on something totally outside their field of expertise, people *will* listen.

CrossFire Guideline #39

It's difficult to ignore people of stature. Even when they have zero knowledge of the subject that they're so critical of.

It's especially common in our society to give undue deference to entertainers and sports stars. Many people will take their side just because they like them or want to be like them.

Stature is very hard to ignore.

Weighing In

There are two kinds of weight. One comes from the actual power that a person or group has over your project. The second comes from a number of people sharing the same viewpoint.

Big Rock

For the first case, a company president's objections regarding a business project will be rarely ignored, while a clerk's may not even be acknowledged. This is due to the officer's control and power over the resources available.

Likewise, a manager that's sponsoring a project has more weight than an even higher ranking manager in a different division.

Big Pile of Little Rocks

On the other hand, numbers can counterbalance individual power. For example, if all the clerks don't like something about a project, only the most stubborn of organizations will ignore them.

CrossFire Guideline #40

As obstacles,
groups can be hard to ignore.
But unlike individuals,
they can often be divided.

This power of numbers allows people in groups, with little weight of their own, to influence goals. The more of them you face, the less likely you'll be able to ignore them.

Nearness

Even in this world of shrinking distances, proximity does have an impact on people's ability to operate as obstacles. The closer they are physically to where the work on the project is being done, the more impact they can have.

CrossFire Guideline #41

The farther away from an obstacle, the easier it is to avoid. This is especially true when the obstacle is a person or group.

This isn't to say that someone can't influence your decisions from a great distance. It's just that it's less likely and more difficult to do.

Whale of a Problem

If your group objects to whaling, protesting at a whaler's offices isn't going to have much of an effect. You're too far away from the action. To increase your effectiveness, you'll need to be out in front of a whaling ship. That's where the real work is done.

(While this might be more *effective, it doesn't necessarily mean that it is* effective. *Other than*

an occasional camera crew, no one but the whalers are going to see your efforts. And it's doubtful you're going to change any of their minds.)

From the whaler's point of view, interfering with the harvest is more of a nuisance than an obstacle. More worrisome to them would be going after the other end of the supply chain. Confronting or educating whale product consumers would probably be more likely to produce the desired effect.

Real Concern

The most logical component of a human obstacle is the legitimacy of their concerns. The more real, tangible, and reasonable their arguments, the fewer grounds you'll have not to address them.

Unfortunately, unless someone incredibly sharp and articulate is involved, you may never see those arguments handed to you in a nice, neat, easy to understand form. I certainly haven't.

CrossFire Guideline #42

Real, tangible concerns need to be addressed. It's insurance against slamming into a camouflaged obstacle ahead.

Instead, you're going to have to probe, interpret, analyze, and sometimes guess at what they're trying to get at. I'm not saying that you have to make their case. But if you see the glimmer of something real, you're going to have to work hard at trying to understand them. Even if they're communicating as if they've got marbles in their mouth.

Of all the components, this is the only one that's fundamentally real. This is not the one to gloss over. If you make a mistake here, you may find yourself heading down a road with the bridge out somewhere ahead. Be smart and read the signs.

Using What You've Got

Road blocks of a logistical nature usually involve some mixture of time, money, and resources (including personnel). These also include any relevant regulatory or competitive limitations.

Every project has to justify its costs against any expected gains from its deployment. Whether it's written down or not doesn't matter. When using the CrossFire method, a financial justification always accompanies any plan. This way if the resources or commitment aren't available, then everyone knows why it's not going to happen.

CrossFire Guideline #43

Logistical limitations force you to prioritize your goals.
Done well, you'll accomplish more than you dreamed. Done badly, you'll accomplish nothing.

Logistics frequently have an impact on even the smallest personal project. Trying to eat and talk at the same time will prove that point.

As the size of the projects grow, it'll become clearer that your resources must be used as sparingly as possible. Success on multiple fronts demands it.

In a very real sense, logistics can be viewed as the governor of all progress. Its imposed limitations make sure that everything doesn't happen simultaneously!

Elevator to the Stars

As an example, it might be technically possible to build a functional, fixed elevator into low earth orbit. It could be used to move items directly from the surface of the earth to a space station in stationary orbit.

At first thought, this might appear impossible. However, if the point on earth and the point in space don't move in relation to each other, it's

---

at least theoretically *possible. Air resistance, gravity, torsional stress, orbital vagaries, solar winds, lunar motion, and other effects would be astonishingly difficult to overcome.*

However, even if technically possible, the logistical resources required to build and maintain such a transport system are too mind-bogglingly high to even contemplate. That is, at least at this time, an insurmountable logistical obstacle.

Mousetrap Construction

Technical issues can vary in complexity from finding a screwdriver to solving a complex issue that has yet to ever occur. As obstacles, if people represent external issues, then technical represents internal ones.

Most technical problems will be discovered as you're working toward your goals. They generally have more to do with your specific approach than with some outsider throwing a wrench into the works.

Your ability to successfully deal with these kinds of obstacles depends not only on the issues involved, but on the skills and knowledge of the resources that you have at your disposal.

Translation: Just because something hasn't been done before, doesn't mean that it can't be done now. The reverse also holds true. Just because someone's done it before doesn't mean your organization can do it now.

CrossFire Guideline #44

Defusing technical obstacles relies more on the skills and knowledge of your resources than on any of the issues involved.

If there are any doubts about whether certain technical elements of a project can be accomplished, their feasibility will have to be proved *before* the rest of the project can be launched.

Pivotal issues, like inventing some new technique or device will, at the very least, have to be theoretically sound and demonstrated on paper before launching any new venture. The greater your realistic confidence that a task can be completed, the lower the risks.

CrossFire Guideline #45

Potential project killing issues need to be at least theoretically resolved before even starting the main effort.

Let's say that you have a working prototype of some innovative gadget. Finding financial backing for such a device is much easier than for someone with just an idea. The substantially lower risk for potential investors is the reason why.

Optimization issues like "Can this computer chip be made to run ten times faster for the same price in the next twelve months?" are less critical. In such a case, if you can substantially meet the overall goal, that *may* be good enough. It'll depend on the organization's particular situation.

Down Lines

Of all the basic types of obstacles, communications problems are the most common and give the biggest headaches. They come in three subtypes: not enough, garbled, and too much.

The first can do the most damage by wasting the greatest amount of available resources. It also can compound the problem by throwing in the frustration of isolation and the fear that something even more terrible may happen.

Broken Connection

When I was in the process of forming Compu-Solve, a successful semi-custom software and computer service bureau, I went to the owner of one of my future competitors for advice.

(Pretty brassy, I know. But what can I say? I was young.)

He was of course very reluctant to tell me anything useful as I peppered him with questions. That is until I asked him one particular question, "What's the biggest problem I'm going to face?"

Taken somewhat aback for a moment, he answered quickly with "Communications."

"Why so?" I asked.

"Because that's your business. You'll need telephone lease lines and dial-in lines for people to access your computers. You'll spend your time talking with prospects to turn them into clients. Your support and development staff will talk with clients, prospects, and between themselves to build and support the systems that the users need."

"Everything you do, every dollar you make, will be as a direct result of communications."

He studied my expression. "I can see that you don't believe me. When I started my business, I asked one of my future competitors the very same things that you're asking me now. He told me the same thing I'm telling you. I didn't believe it either. But you will. The first time you lose your telephone connections, you'll know it's true."

(This was before email, fax machines, cell phones, or the myriad of alternative communication devices available now.)

Four weeks after we started operations, we suddenly lost all connectivity and communications. We were down hard. While waiting for them to be repaired, each passing tick of the clock made my blood pressure increase. Six hours later we came back up. The first call I made was to apologize for ever doubting him. All I heard from the other end of the line was laughter.

Solid communication is not necessarily better than none at all. If it becomes garbled or misunderstood, there's the very real danger that large amounts of your resources may be wasted. In critical situations it's always wise to get confirmation of what's going to take place or at least have the ability to monitor progress.

The last subtype, excessive communications, is the least worrisome of the bunch. It's generally a symptom of you or someone else is doubting that an assigned task will be executed properly.

While this can result in wasted resources, it's usually on a smaller scale. If it continues to occur over an extended period, it's probably a confidence or education problem that needs to be addressed.

Regardless of the type of communications obstacles you face, fewer will appear when you use competent people with well-defined responsibilities and give them the power to act. You'll rarely be disappointed.

CrossFire Guideline #46

*Obstacles from too much, too little,
or garbled communications
are the most common
and the least necessary.*

False savings from using poorly qualified personnel or engaging in micromanagement wastes huge amounts of resources. Don't be the one to create an obstacle breeding ground. Fighting your own actions is the most futile activity of all.

Source of Trouble

Creating a trail through unknown territory isn't always easy. Obstacles will litter your path. Some will be easy to predict. Others won't appear until you're right on top of them.

Recovering quickly from an obstacle that suddenly pops up requires you to be able to identify them instantly. Now you can.

For review purposes, the obstacles you'll face come from four sources:

√ People

√ Logistics

√ Technical

√ Communications

CrossFire Guideline #47

Obstacles are derived from four sources: people, logistics, technical, and communications.

You've learned what the source of each of them are, what aspects makes them obstacles, and what effects you can expect when they occur. In other words, you know everything that's required to successfully neutralize them.

It's up to you to make them go away. ♦

Preview

Wooden obstacles

Six ways out

Going faster by going slower

What's important enough to do

New requirements

Low effort navigation

Dealing with issues

When to stop

The possibilities

Online Supplement

www.IntegritysImpact.com/ObstacleHandling

Chapter 5

Clearing the Road

"If everything seems under control, you're just not going fast enough."

—Mario Andretti

E LIMINATING obstacles can take some finesse. Just pushing them around doesn't get rid of them. It just wastes a lot of your time and effort. In the last chapter we covered the types of obstacles that you'll usually run across. Here, we use that knowledge to take an active approach in dealing with them.

Your Trusty Steamroller

A good analogy for handling the obstacles in your path to success might be to think of them as the problems you'd have when building a road through a small forest.

After identifying a reasonable course for the new road, dealing with the trees comes next. This includes all parts of the tree: leaves, branches, trunk, stump, and roots.

The roots like some kinds of obstacles are often mistakenly left in place. When ignored, these invisible and hard to deal with pieces will eventually break even the strongest road.

As building progresses, the route is in some flux. It moves and changes as the needs and opportunities dictate. These fine adjustments minimize the effort required to complete it.

CrossFire Guideline #48

*In use, even the best plan
constantly changes.*

Each tree along the way will need to be examined within the overall scope of where the road is trying to go. Then you can determine how best to get past the ones in your way.

When faced with the inevitable problems and issues on the road to your dreams, the following guidelines will help simplify your choices and let you decide how best to proceed.

Armed with a measuring tape and a sharp axe, go to it!

Siding with You

Like the number of faces on any cube, there are six different ways to handle any obstacle. Five are readily apparent, and the sixth is usually hidden from view.

The visible ones are: delaying it (for a time), ignoring it, integrating it, avoiding it, and resolving it. The final one, the one that no one wants to talk about, I'll save for last.

Take Five

Not all things need to be done immediately. Most of the time you're free to select the best or most convenient time to do a particular task. This ability to rearrange your schedule or delay for a short period can be a powerful ally in succeeding with any project. It also can reduce the stress from being unnecessarily rigid in your approach.

If you're unsure how best to attack a task and you feel that a little time will help, consider delaying. The extra time for thought might allow you to develop a better idea of exactly what needs to be done, instead of just spinning your wheels.

However, if the delay is unlikely to result in a significant reduction in effort you might as well dive in. In such a case postponement is just procrastination. It won't help your cause. It'll just hurt it.

CrossFire Guideline #49

*Wisely delaying a task
eliminates the stress of
missing false deadlines,
while minimizing wasted effort.
Unwisely, it's just procrastination.*

As detailed in a subsection of the next chapter (see "Delaying Tactics" starting on page 146), postponing action on a particular item may reap sound benefits. Just be sure to act prudently and follow the given guidelines.

Another good reason for delaying a task is to allow you to finish another one first, if it makes sense to do so. Like assembling a bicycle, putting the gears on the rear wheel before you put it on the frame saves you time and effort. Jumping the gun and putting the wheel on first without the gears is just a poor use of your resources.

Icy Dreams, Part 1

(This story is broken up into six pieces to illustrate all the ways you can deal with obstacles.)

In the summer before college, four of my closest friends and I decided that we needed to do something dramatic before we all went off to our various colleges. After much debate, we decided climbing Mount McKinley in Alaska was just the ticket. That would be impressive.

We all had backpacking, rock climbing, and snow/ice experience. Several of us had even graduated from Yosemite's rock climbing school. Besides, it was the highest mountain we could all afford to get to.

Over the next month or so we did research, got the best topographical maps (with a huge blank area on the south side of the mountain labeled "Unexplored"), planned out our route, prepared the sacrificial car (3000 miles of gravel road wasn't going to be kind to it), bought equipment, packed carefully, and even did a trial run in Yosemite. It was early August, and we were ready.

Since the start time wasn't absolutely critical, we delayed a week to let me earn an additional paycheck from pumping gas and for another one of us to convince his parent to let him go.

The week passed, and flush with eighty dollars in my pocket, I was ready. My friend wasn't so lucky. He couldn't get past his parent's "it's too dangerous/frivolous" argument. Running out of time, we left without him.

Leaving earlier would've only allowed three of us to go. Delaying a little gave us the possibility of expanding our group up to five. We ended up with four—an increase of 33%. An improvement that proved critical to our survival later on.

Thunk, Thunk

Ignoring a problem can be a valid way of dealing with it. Choosing correctly what can be dismissed is something that's based mostly on your experience. Experience in understanding what's important and what's not for a given project.

CrossFire Guideline #50

There are exactly two legitimate reasons to ignore an issue. It either doesn't significantly impact the project or you've got no other choice.

It's very difficult to give you a simple checklist to use in these cases. So, beginning troubleshooters should err on the side of caution and, if possible, rely on the guidance of others with more experience with this type of project.

Of course if no one's ever successfully done what you're trying to accomplish, your guess is probably as good as anyone else's.

As you gain experience, you'll develop an intuitive understanding what needs have to be addressed and what can be safely ignored. The better your judgement gets in this area, the more successful you'll become. As an added benefit, you'll also be able to produce tighter and more accurate schedules and estimates.

Icy Dreams, Part 2

Trying to make up for lost time, we drove very fast and around the clock. We made it from San Francisco to Seattle in only ten hours (850 miles). Crossing the border into Canada, our pace quickened even more.

Even on the gravel Alaskan Highway the speedometer rarely read below 100 mph. Everyone drove. Everyone made mistakes. We all survived. Amazing.

Somewhere in Northwest Territories, the car stalled and wouldn't restart. Three of us poked and prodded the engine. Then we checked the electrical system. No luck.

Finding the closest mile marker, we discovered that the nearest gas station was 125 miles behind us and who knew how far in front of us. Argh!

Mike Dreese, knowing nothing about automobiles, had watched our futile efforts to resuscitate the car. Stepping up to the engine with a smile, he soundly hit the air cleaner with a rolled up copy of the Wall Street Journal. *He demanded that the car start. Scott Sorensen tried it. The engine roared to life.*

Having little choice on whether or not to trust Mike's "repair," we decided to ignore the problem. We were off again.

Amazingly enough, the "fix" held all the way to Anchorage.

Permanent Detour

Occasionally an apparent obstacle isn't one at all. Instead, it's a requirement. The reasons are just so strong for its incorporation into the project that it's absolutely necessary to address it for the project to be truly successful.

Usually this happens in the early stages of planning. Some critical piece of information comes into your possession from an unusual source. Of course, you had no clue it was out there. Often it's surprising in nature or scope.

In a business environment this frequently happens when interviewing a key manager that you didn't expect to have much of a say in how your project was to be structured. Instead, his needs end up dramatically impacting it. With this type of obstacle it just gets assimilated into the project.

CrossFire Guideline #51

*Sometimes requirements
are disguised as obstacles.
Not integrating them can be
damaging or even fatal
to the project.*

Icy Dreams, Part 3

The Alaskan border was our next big hurdle. Seeing four 18-year-olds with long hair and backpacks was obviously too much for the customs agents to resist. They jump on us like hungry wolves. Our backpacks and the car were torn apart. We were there for hours.

We asked what they were looking for. They said drugs. Pretty amusing since at the time drugs were legal in Alaska and were being smuggled from there into Canada—not the other way around.

Customs refused to accept that nothing sneaky was going on. At one point in the process, one of the border guards said to the

other "Hey look Harry, film in a film canister."
They laughed. We grumbled.

With nothing to find they eventually let us go.
Mt. McKinley (currently called Denali) National
Park was finally in striking range.

Arriving early in the morning at the park, we
quickly applied for our wilderness permits.
They were just as quickly denied. We were
stunned.

We then found out that you had to ask permission of the Air Force to climb McKinley. We
were dumbfounded. It seemed they were the
only ones with a helicopter that could fly high
enough to do any rescue if we got in trouble. No
permission, no permit. Rats!

Eager to save our mission, Bruce Bothwell
and I quizzed the Rangers. We soon found out
that there were bigger problems than just the
permit. The most practical route up the mountain went through Gunsight Pass. It was blocked
by a recent avalanche. Going around it would
take time that we didn't have to spare. The only
other reasonable approach across the glaciers
had just days before nearly swallowed an entire
team of climbers down a crevasse. Argh!

(Historically 1974 was a terrible year for
weather related climbing conditions in McKinley
Park. No year in the three decades since has
been so treacherous.)

Due to the mountain's then current appetite
for climbers, we applied for a permit to climb

one of the lower peaks. It seemed the Air Force didn't care about those (even though they were still high enough that they'd be doing any rescue). Our request was granted with an understanding wink from the issuing Ranger, and we left.

Modifying our stated goal didn't significantly change the magnitude or importance of what we had set out to accomplish. It simply was an adjustment required by the reality of the situation.

Making a Turn

Avoidance is the low effort method for dealing with obstacles. Like driving a car, missing an object in the road is easier the farther away you see it. Noticed far enough in advance, only a slight correction of the wheel will be required. Seen at the last moment, even a severe jerk to the side won't guarantee you miss it.

The amount of any turn required will be dictated by the size of the obstacle and your proximity to it. As an example, if the manager of your department hates surprises and tends to lash out when they happen, it would be best to inform him of any possible problems long before they might happen. Careful planning on your part and a long horizon will make this easy. In an immediate and urgent crisis, you'll find this much harder to accomplish.

CrossFire Guideline #52

*Imagining what can go wrong,
how to fix it, and
when it might occur determines
your ability to avoid problems.
Preparation is over half the battle.*

With all projects the goal is to try and see potential problems and issues long before they become significant. This way you can build in allowances or fine-tune your plans well in advance. That will keep them from delaying or impacting the project in any significant way.

Icy Dreams, Part 4

With the permit in hand, we waited for a bus to take us to the midstation, some eighty miles away. After a couple of hours, we finally arrived at where we'd start our approach.

Scanning south from the Ranger's station, we were on a ridge overlooking the McKinley River with its myriad of braids. On the other side were foothills leading up to the glacier. Mt. McKinley itself disappeared into the clouds.

On those same foothills we could see what appeared to be several large vehicles. Upon closer inspection with the binoculars, we realized that those weren't cars, but Grizzly bears. Those animals were huge. We unanimously decided to avoid that entire area.
How very reasonable of us.

Potholes

Not all obstacles can be seen in advance, nor even exist until you get to them. They just suddenly appear in what was a clear smooth road. Your first indication of a problem might be a loud bang and your car (project) swerving unexpectedly.

After a project has progressed for a while, people with new objections may appear. Though they are often passionate and vocal about their views, it's not always apparent that their proposed changes will need to be integrated into it. That's for you to decide.

Though not straightforward, if they raise legitimate issues, the project may need to address them. This will require you to resolve them.

The other methods for dealing with obstacles that we've discussed involve working with them as a whole. In their entirety. In this case, resolution will require a close examination of all the components involved. Each piece may require a mixture of the various techniques, plus a healthy dose of compromise by all parties.

This is where most of the real work takes place. Keeping a level head, a reasonable pace, and solid view of the project's important overall goals will get you and the project through these difficult parts. You'll both be better because of it.

CrossFire Guideline #53

Compromise and a variety of techniques are often required to resolve obstacles. This is where the real work of turning dreams into reality is done.

Icy Dreams, Part 5

Working our way down the ridge, we quickly came to the McKinley River. It braided into many strands that averaged about three to four feet deep. The depth wasn't a problem, but its temperature and bottom were.

The water was the cloudy blue color of glacier runoff. You couldn't see the bottom. It was also only about three degrees above freezing. Having not planned on a river crossing, we took off our shoes and held them and our packs up high, walking on the four to eight inch diameter pebble-like stones covering the river bed.

Painful, slippery, and mind numbingly cold, we eventually crossed all the braids and got to the other side. Then it started to rain. Hard.

As we put our shoes back on, we modified our goal again. Now we just wanted to get onto the permanent glacier. That was enough. We were all freezing. All our preparations had been for snow and ice—not rivers and rain.

Climbing from the river bed up to the top of the bordering hills was hard. The effect of being soaked in the freezing water was taking its toll. The pain was becoming very pronounced. We changed the goal again. We just wanted to see the glacier.

Finally reaching the crest, we realized that it wasn't a crest at all. Even though it flattened out, it was really just the end of the dirt portion of the mountain. We stood at the base of the glacier. We had achieved more than our modified goal.

Icy blue. Bright even in the early evening sun. The glacier curved up the face of the mountain. It called to us.

At that exact same moment of bliss, we got hit in the face with a sixty-knot wind straight off the ice. Suddenly we were four flash-frozen popsicles.

As each new issue cropped up, we just dealt with it. Simple. No complaining. No worrying. No excuses. We may have been frozen, but we weren't stressed out about it.

CrossFire Guideline #54

*True goals are often intangible.
Stated goals, meant to visibly
demonstrate success,
can often be changed
without altering the true ones.*

Road's End

The last face on our six-sided cube is hidden from view. It's facing down for a reason. Every project manager hates to admit that it even exists: quitting.

This can indeed be a bitter pill to take, especially for entrepreneurs. Having been told over and over again by their peers to persevere, persevere, persevere they're the least likely to know when it's really time to pack it in.

Looking back on one of the successful companies that I started long ago, I remember a director on my board asking the same question at every meeting. "Is it time to sell yet?" he'd ask. Even so when it came time to sell the company, I just couldn't see it.

When the boulder in the project's path is so immense, so overwhelming, that there's no way for the project to continue, then quitting is the only reasonable choice left. Cut your losses and kill the project (hopefully salvaging anything of value).

Maybe time will erode that insurmountable rock down to a manageable size. Just make sure before you quit that you didn't overlook some piece of dynamite that could be used to turn that rock into a manageable pile of rubble.

Say, does anyone have a match?

CrossFire Guideline #55

Quitting when faced with an unsurmountable and unavoidable obstacle isn't failure. It's rational.

Icy Dreams, Part 6

Looking to get out of the wind, we tried to set up camp. The severe wind, pelting rain, and rocky soil conspired to make any such attempt impossible. Beaten, we gave up and decided to head back toward the now closed midstation.

Remember that this was summertime in Alaska, very near the Arctic Circle. Even though it was around nine at night, the sun was still up. Even after the sun dropped below the horizon, it still wouldn't be very dark outside. Instead, it would be a kind of eerie twilight.

Down the hills with our sixty to seventy pound packs, we made rapid progress back to the river. Once there no one was anxious to tiptoe through that cold water again. But having no other choice, off came the shoes and we forded the braids again.

Once having crossed the river for the second time in five hours, the cold was becoming unbearable. All of us were showing various signs of hypothermia. It took a strong focus on the perceived safety of the midstation, which wasn't yet visible, to keep going.

As we climbed up the ridge, Scott and Bruce were suffering the most. Finally, about a thousand feet from the top, Scott said he could go no farther. "Leave me behind" he said. Bruce wanted to stop too.

Mike and I, barely lucid ourselves, understood that staying could well mean dying. We split most of Scott's pack between the two of us. Prodding Bruce and dragging Scott, we eventually made it to the top and then on to the ranger's midstation. God, that was hard.

It wasn't long after we arrived back home in California and the pain faded that we realized that climbing the mountain had never been the real goal. It was the making of memories.

On that score, we had succeeded gloriously. As a project, we failed dismally at our initial goal. In the end though, what we salvaged was far better than we had ever hoped for.

Everything You've Got

On that trip we used every obstacle handling technique available. We delayed, we ignored, we avoided, we resolved, and we quit. Along the way we set goals, added goals, modified goals, achieved goals, and gave up on goals.

For quick reference and review, use the following list to deal with any obstacles you encounter:

√ **Delay**—temporarily suspend work on the obstacle. This will allow time for one of the techniques below to be more easily used to deal with the obstacle or for a clearer understanding of exactly what's involved to resolve it.

√ **Ignore**—do nothing because the obstacle is outside the scope of the project (it's a problem, but not one that has to be dealt with for the project to be successful). No changes are made to the project.

√ **Avoid**—make changes (hopefully minor) to the project to prevent having to deal with the obstacle. This is like ignoring, but the modifications to the project are meant to drive the obstacle outside the project's scope instead of resolving it.

√ **Integrate**—merge not only the requirements for dealing with the obstacle into the project's goals, but incorporate the obstacle's goals as well. The obstacle isn't an obstacle after all. Its needs are the project's needs.

√ **Resolve**—use a combination of the above methods plus compromise to deal with the obstacle. Breaking it down into smaller, more manageable pieces is a frequent approach.

√ **Quit**—kill the project because the obstacle is insurmountable and unavoidable. There's no way to successfully complete the project with the resources and time available.

CrossFire Guideline #56
Vague goals get vague results. *Get what you really want* *by visualizing your goals clearly* *and in great detail.*

With respect to the climbing trip, we were all over the map in our effectiveness. This was mostly due to our rather vague initial goal (doing something dramatic) and our almost zero resources (a car, gas, and four strong wills) to achieve it.

Still, the trip was wonderful. May all your failures be as glorious. ♦

Preview

Leadership's purpose
Motivators
Dealing with isolation
Vision versus pressure
Whom to trust
Stamina to succeed
Finding yourself when lost
Compromising on perfection
Mistakes were made

Online Supplement

www.IntegritysImpact.com/Leadership

Chapter 6

Head of the Pack

"First they ignore you, then they laugh at you, then they fight you, then you win."

—Mahatma Gandhi

GOOD leadership skills are often ignored. What people do notice are *bad* leadership skills. This is one of those cases where "praise is the absence of criticism for a short period of time." If you want to succeed in business, strong leadership skills aren't an option—they're a requirement.

> ## CrossFire Guideline #57
>
> *Good leadership skills aren't*
> *much of an advantage in life.*
> *However, bad ones are*
> *a very big disadvantage.*

Leadership, like life, goes on even when we're not paying attention. With all the various distractions we're faced with when in any leadership role, it's easy to stray from the proper course. That's only natural. Getting back on course is the part that takes special effort.

Picking Up a Coin

You can look at leadership as a coin. On one side is knowledge and on the other is the ability to motivate. Knowing how to solve problems will be supplied by your own experience and CrossFire. The motivational side is a bit harder.

People are primary motivated by three things: fear, belief, and desire. (Actually some experts argue that only fear exists and that the others are just fear in disguise. They maybe right.)

Check out any ad and you'll see what I mean. Whether it's selling cars, charitable donations, newspapers, hair color, insurance, or anything else you can think of, they all use one or more of the three motivators. Without them, few of us would ever act and the ad (as well as society) would be a total failure.

| **CrossFire Guideline #58** |
| *The most important skill of an effective leader is the ability to motivate others.* |

A good leader knows how to assemble the right motivation for a given group of people in a particular situation.

Making Things Happen

Leaders shoulder the responsibility for making things happen. Their job is to guide those involved toward a particular goal. How well they do is heavily dependent on their experience and knowledge of what to do when things start to go wrong.

| **CrossFire Guideline #59** |
| *Great leaders take responsibility for the actions of themselves and those they lead. Be a great leader.* |

The next few sections take a look at some of the more common pitfalls regularly faced by all levels of managers. There are many other problems that leaders have to deal with, but these few are the source of most crises. For each we'll examine the symptoms, the root problem, the more common causes, the possible outcomes if left unchecked, and ways to effectively defuse them.

(For standard leadership concepts and detailed instructions on becoming a leader, I'll refer you to the many outstanding books and classes that are available. The subject is well described elsewhere and just too big to cover adequately here.)

Using What You Learn

As a manager, you can use your new understanding to avoid situations that trip up even experienced leaders. This will give you an edge in the workplace.

Even when your leadership isn't required, the following information will still be useful. It'll help you ensure the best possible chance for achieving your goals. With it you can detect the early warning signs of a leader or manager who's in trouble.

You can then use your knowledge of the problem and what causes it to help extract management from their predicament. This way the project avoids the heavy costs and huge delays that are typically associated with such failures.

You don't mind being the hero, do you?

Lone Wolf

Isolation and the accompanying loneliness is, hands down, the number one pitfall for leaders. It's absolutely rampant in top positions where a lot rides on every decision. People often found in this state are corporate officers, military commanders, small business owners, heads of emergency services groups, and many, many others. Even individuals and single parents often fall into this trap.

It's slow and insidious in its progression. Each of us is only able to take so much before falling victim to its effects.

Working in Isolation

The problem grows straight out of the isolation that people feel, whether real or imagined. They can't confide in those that they work with or are close to. The reasons tend to be practical, but no less hard to endure. Some examples:

• *The physically isolated submarine captain. The captain's command (the crew of the boat) needs to feel confident that he knows exactly what to do at all times—even when he doesn't.*

- *The mentally isolated market maker in the stock market. He needs to compile and process thousands of pieces of information, many seemingly unimportant, about the business sector he works on to give his company an edge over its competitors.*

- *The socially isolated AIDS sufferer trying to live a normal life. He feels that he mustn't confide his problems dealing with the virus to those he works with, so he can avoid tainting their relationships with him.*

All of these barriers leave each of them with few, if any, people that they can really talk to.

Being basically social creatures, humans don't do well when they can't communicate with others. We use almost all of our senses: sight, sound, smell, and touch to pick up on what others are trying to communicate. We really *want* to connect with them.

All of us work and feel better when we have the opportunity (whether we use it or not) to question ourselves using a trusted person's insight. It's a rare individual indeed that can't use an occasional "Atta boy!" or a "Whoa, are you crazy?" to give life some perspective.

CrossFire Guideline #60

Avoid isolation.
Find someone to confide in.

When left alone (literally), the person's basic instincts will tend to amplify to possibly frightening levels. If cautious, they'll reach the point of inaction. If proactive, they may become reckless. If creative, they'll produce nonsense. If a fast mover, they'll start running over people and the rules.

Who knows how a particular person will react? Defusing the problem early or avoiding it altogether is the best solution.

In the cases outlined above, the situations are pretty fixed and there's not a lot that can be done to break down the barriers. So what do you do if you find yourself stuck in a similar situation? Try going outside of the environment for support.

Use friends, family, spouses, bosses, or people with similar jobs in different industries. Even total strangers can work given the right situation. Many times all you need to do is just talk while feeling that someone's listening to you. (The majority of most psychiatrists' and psychoanalysts' patients are just people who want a friendly ear to listen to them.)

If you're not in quite such an extreme situation, just cautiously reaching out to others might do the trick. Often we isolate ourselves out of fear. Fear of getting hurt, fear of losing face, fear of the unknown. Take a chance on yourself and others. Reach out and connect with someone—anyone.

Blinders

Solving large or complex problems requires a certain amount of creativity and open-mindedness. Without them, the final results will suffer from a serious lack of vision. The project might find itself in jeopardy. To paraphrase an old quote, "A fool is someone who expects things to change by doing the same old thing." Evaluating the situation with unassuming eyes is your mandate.

CrossFire Guideline #61

Some habits will have to be broken to see with new eyes.

Unfortunately everyone has blind spots. We get comfortable with the way things are and tend to be less than enthusiastic about changes. Okay. We're human. We *hate* change.

In each of us is the innate ability to quickly form new habits. Habits can be good. They let us do things without even thinking about them. Just like driving down the road listening to the radio. Suddenly, you realize that you can't remember the last few miles. That's habits for you. Good for the repetitive, bad for the creative. They're blinders that can really limit your vision of a better future.

There are many other causes for a serious lack of vision. First on the list maybe that your job has just never really required it. A long time production line worker is generally not going to be the person to talk to about getting ideas about radically improving production capacity. However, they *will* be experts in making incremental improvements to the line.

These kinds of improvements will fine-tune the operation, but rarely lead to major (20+%) enhancements. For really big improvements (50–500+%), a totally new approach will usually be required.

Other causes of selective blindness can be:

• Corporate political pressure (we don't do that here)

• Social pressure (we don't want to)

• Ignorance (haven't seen it any other way)

• Money (we've got zero budget for this)

- Time (we've got no time for this)

- Priorities (we've got more important things to do)

- Personal preferences (I hate that idea)

Plus many others. These limitations are a natural part of the process. The key is to not let them adversely affect the exploration portion of the project. This is where open-mindedness needs to reign supreme. Limitations might reappear when deciding on the final solution, but that's to be expected.

When it comes to an important goal, you need to question everything. Nothing is sacred. Nothing is obvious. You need to see things for what they really are.

CrossFire Guideline #62

Questioning the unquestionable is usually the only way to make giant leaps toward your goals.

You desperately want to avoid the King's clothes syndrome where everyone sees the king is naked, but no one is willing to say so. Instead, you want to be like the little boy who states the obvious, "He's got no clothes on!"

If they fire you for it, oh well. If they can't handle the truth, you'll probably be a lot better off (and happier) somewhere else.

This level of evenhandedness can be exceedingly difficult if you've worked somewhere for a long period of time. In that situation you'll have to *pretend* you know nothing.

(For those of you considering a full-time career in business analysis, it's one of the few fields where the less preconceptions you have about a particular situation, the better off you are. Knowing too much in the beginning makes it very difficult for most people to actively test widely held assumptions. No one likes to appear foolish.)

Through the Mirror Darkly

There are few absolutes in life. Even truth can be open to interpretation. Multiple eyewitnesses to a crime will often give radically different accounts of what happened. Each one could be telling the absolute truth *through their eyes*. In other words, from their perspective.

Truth is always colored by a person's experience, attitudes, knowledge, and beliefs. Even when dealing with a single person, there are always three witnesses. It's that group of people that you see when you look in the mirror—me, myself, and I.

CrossFire Guideline #63

*Everyone, and that means
each and every human,
sees things from their own
unique perspective.*

Let me introduce you to these three diverse people looking back at you.

Reflection number one is the person you want others to see. This person can change from moment to moment. They're unreliable at best.

Reflection number two is the person you wish you were. This person tends to change very slowly. Unless you've experienced substantial traumatic events in your life, it has probably changed very little since you were a young adult.

The last reflection is the real, unpolished, unadorned, and unvarnished you. This is your private self.

CrossFire Guideline #64

*Your first and primary confidant
is always your private self.*

Talking to Yourself

When making important decisions, you'll need an absolute confidant. Someone whom you can trust

implicitly. This is going to be the person that you
check every idea, concept, and plan with first and
last. It's got to be you—your private self.

This you, the one who knows *everything*
about you, is who you should measure the outside world against. Not the other two. When you
start using them to gauge reality, that's when you
start lying to yourself.

Deceiving yourself can really foul up achieving
your goals. The impact can be devastating. In a
high pressure environment, there may also be a
strong temptation to alter your decisions to affect
how others perceive you. That's a killer.

It's like trying to build a house on quick sand.
You'll be lucky to nail two boards together before
you and the boards disappear from sight. Not exactly the result that you're looking for.

Instead, when faced with difficult or important
decisions, double-check your motivation. Ask
yourself a single question: Is what I'm considering
truly in the best interests of the company and the
project?

If not, something's wrong. Fix it.

A "C" Is Not a Circle

Great ideas and great plans are worthless if you
or your organization doesn't have the stamina
and determination to follow them through to completion. Partially done doesn't count. Projects are

strange beasts. The last 10% of the project takes 90% of the effort. (Which also means that tasks *always* look easier than they really are.)

In other words, it may look like you're nearing the end of the tunnel, when in reality you've just been digging in the dirt. To get through to the other side will require blasting through thick, solid, unforgiving slabs of granite.

There are many roadblocks to getting to the end of any project. Some come from lack of resources. Others are from changes in key personnel. Still others appear from an apparent change in organizational priorities. Most, however, come from a simple lack of will. The will to follow through.

Laziness and procrastination always win by default. Unless you and others use your power to champion a project, it has no hope of ever being completed.

CrossFire Guideline #65

*A well planned, finished project
is worth more than ten times
the value of one 90% completed.*

Bringing projects to their full completion is very difficult. There are times that a project may be terminated early for good reason, but those reasons shouldn't include being too boring or tedious to finish (everyone hates tying up loose ends).

Just like with a jigsaw puzzle, leaving out the last few pieces may allow you to see the big picture, but it's not nearly as satisfying or appealing to everyone as when all the pieces are in place.

Also any missing pieces could cause major frustrations and headaches in unexpected ways. They may be severe enough to unravel the entire project.

Remember that the original plan was developed in its entirety for a reason and no one really knows the true effects of casually dropping components. Avoid the temptation to cut and run.

Wandering Off

You can get into even more trouble by getting lost along the way. I'm not talking about losing your way down some corridor of the company you're currently working for, but losing sight of the goals that you're trying to achieve. This can happen even when the project appears to everyone involved to be zooming right along. Too bad activity doesn't necessarily mean progress.

Regardless of the reason, it's during these periods of standing still when your project's resources (time, money, people) can be consumed at an alarming rate. (There seems to be some inverse law about projects that says that the less that gets done per hour, the more that hour will cost.) Controlling these useless delays is one of the keys to minimizing cost and time overruns.

CrossFire Guideline #66

Getting lost can be very expensive.
Avoid the cost.
Check your progress
toward your goals often.

Getting lost can happen for a variety of reasons. Most of the time it's due to poor planning, but that's not the only way. Sometimes it can be caused for the opposite reason—being too heavily focused on the process (plan) instead of the goals. This can lead to some strange results.

Say Cheese

Let's say that your organization is in the business of selling sandwiches to fast-food stores. Because you make pretty good sandwiches, you need a better way to track the sales and distribution of these fast sellers.

You look around the marketplace for some system to address your needs and you find zip. With careful deliberation and planning you start a project to create one that will meet your needs. Great! Now the problem.

Six months into this one year project, some cheese salesman walks into your office and casually mentions what a competitor of yours has been doing lately. They've just deployed their own custom system for tracking their burritos, and it's working like a champ. It even does 95% of what your project is trying to accomplish.

Not only that, he tells you, but they want to recoup some of their development costs, so they're planning to sell licenses to use their system cheap. If you buy theirs, it'll cost you less than half of what you're going to spend in the next six months! Argh!

If true, what do you do?

Unbelievably, nine times out of ten, the project manager will ignore the information and continue with their own in-house project. Bad idea. A very bad idea. Can you think of some reasons why they might do that? Take a moment and think about it. Then read on and see some of the excuses.

The only valid reason to continue with your project is if you don't believe what you've been told. No other reason works. If you decide to ignore them you better be very, very sure that they're wrong. It's only prudent. After all, you're betting your job and maybe your career on your decision.

Your extraordinary level of caution is required because the potential cost of you being wrong by not participating is just too over-whelming. Let's take a look at just the first few reasons that come to mind:

- Using your competitor's solution saves half the remaining budgeted dollars for the project (less expense) over the next six months—money that could be better used to increase the marketing or production budgets (more sales).

- The personnel resources involved, including management's mental bandwidth, will be free to concentrate on selling more sandwiches more efficiently (less expense, more sales).

- You get to totally dodge the possibility, even if remote, that your project fails (less risk).

- The quality of the final system will be that much greater (more users) and more stable with multiple companies using it (less risk).

- You don't lose market share to your competitor because they have their system up and you're still waiting for yours (more sales).

- *No long-term headaches of supporting a custom in-house system (less risk and expense).*

- *Worse case, you could always resurrect the project, if something unforeseen makes the new system go away (less risk).*

Anyway you measure it, continuing your project is a poor idea. Whether it's personal ego, difficulty in admitting that the first half of the project was a wasted effort (think of it as risk avoidance—even if you did know about their project, they could've failed), corporate pride ("These guys make a lousy burrito, how would it look if we bought their system?"), or too tight a focus on the plan instead of the goals, you need to bite the bullet and buy the license.

Like everything in life the change in approach might be a disaster, but continuing with your project when faced with a better solution would definitely be one.

(In reality, even if the installed price of their system was two or three times the expected cost to finish your project, it probably would still be a good idea because the gains from the distributed risk and more users.)

CrossFire Guideline #67

*Keeping one eye focused on
your goal allows you to
take advantage of any reasonable
shortcuts that suddenly appear.*

Delaying Tactics

Some reasons for losing your way can be more subtle. One that tends to eat lots of resources is having a particularly difficult problem suddenly pop up. Unless the problem is a show stopper (you can't continue the project unless you fix it first), put it aside and come back to it later.

As long as you don't forget that it's still out there, the delay could actually be helpful. The problem may solve itself, you'll think of a solution, or it may just go away.

CrossFire Guideline #68

*Sometimes delaying pieces of a
project can speed up the overall
progress toward your goals.*

Just like working on a jigsaw puzzle. Put down the piece and pickup another. Even the most difficult to place piece is easy if you wait until you're nearly done. Then you'll see just how obvious the fit becomes.

(Be careful to avoid using this delaying technique too much. It can cause even more severe problems when used to excess. As a rule of thumb, you shouldn't have more than 5–10% of the outstanding tasks delayed at any one time. If more is needed, you might need to adjust your approach.)

Common detours, like lack of good planning, underfunding, unrealistic deadlines, and others, should be taken care of by the proper use of CrossFire. Many more can be dealt with by just checking your project's current course regularly against the goals for the project. Remember the final destination is the important part—not the trip.

Lack of Recognizable Landmarks

Going off in the wrong direction or becoming distracted happens occasionally to everybody who manages long-term projects. What's amazing, really amazing, is how few people really know what they're doing. Solving nonsimple business problems involving people isn't an easy task. Huge cost and time overruns, as well as spectacular failures, are a common outcome.

After reading this book and others in the series on the CrossFire method, this particular pitfall should disappear. This doesn't mean that there won't be times when you're unsure of which way to go. But you'll have the tools in hand to make an educated guess and the ability to tell quickly whether your "guess" is right or wrong.

CrossFire Guideline #69

*The most efficient order
for completing the tasks
in a project will often change
as you progress.*

Armed with that knowledge, you can adjust your course accordingly. The technique, the *method*, will keep you from being lost for long. Just like navigators for thousands of years have used their experience, maps, the stars, the moon, and the sun to find their way home, you can use your experience and CrossFire. Even in unfamiliar seas, you'll know how to get to the next destination.

The Immovable Object

If you work at some goal long enough and hard enough, at some point in the process you're going to have a vision. A vision of a solution that addresses most, if not all, of your problems.

What you envision may be elegant, beautiful, simple, practical, or even sexy. Remember that thought, because that's not what you're going to get. If you're fortunate, the final result will have some faint resemblance to what you saw. Anything more is just icing on the cake. Get over it and move on.

CrossFire Guideline #70

Dreams aren't reality.
Rarely does achieving a goal
exactly match
how you envisioned it.

Stake in the Ground

Other times you may be required to take a stand. At these key turning points, getting an important feature or approach built into the project could have a large impact on a project's usefulness and success. These are times when you push hard for your ideas. Just don't become fixated on a single approach. Remain flexible.

If someone is pushing equally hard in another direction, then you'll need to understand *why* they're doing so. See if their needs are valid. If so, try to incorporate their requirements into the final solution. Compromise. Don't try to run over your opponents. In a shoving match, you may be the one that ends up on the ground flattened—not your foe.

> ## CrossFire Guideline #71
>
> *Stand up for your beliefs.*
> *If you don't,*
> *why should anyone else?*

Wrong Way Corrigan

Unlike the famous pilot who in 1938 filed a flight plan for New York to California and then ended up in Dublin, Ireland a day later (where he *really* wanted to go in the first place, but he couldn't get permission), most people don't deliberately try to get things wrong.

Let's recap the most common leadership errors. They are:

√ Isolating yourself from others

√ Lack of vision

√ Failing to follow through

√ Going off on a tangent

√ Not knowing what you're doing

√ Being inflexible

√ Fooling yourself

√ Not standing up for important goals

Avoiding these pitfalls will help make you a stronger leader. When you find your progress slowing down or things not going well, check yourself against this list first. With a little luck, the area you're having a problem with will be obvious. Stomp the fire out quickly, before it gets out of control. ♦

Preview

Vanishing limitations
Surviving your choices
Sensing the possibilities
Seconds like hours
Connection to the world
Focusing your power
Razor sharpness
Three lenses
Combination effects

Online Supplement

www.IntegritysImpact.com/Results

Chapter 7

Hidden Assets

"People become really quite remarkable when they start thinking that they can do things. When they believe in themselves they have the first secret of success."

—Norman Vincent Peale

A STRANGE and wondrous thing happens when you're faced with sudden and terrible danger. In less than half a heartbeat, your mind and body go into survival mode. A heavy shot of adrenaline is dumped into your bloodstream, while every fiber of your being comes to grips with the crisis at hand.

You've just entered the upper stratosphere of human performance. Unbelievable feats of physical prowess and mental acrobats are possible, and even likely here.

Full Power

In such situations, each and every one of your self-imposed limitations vanishes. All the usual rules are thrown out. Almost anything that you can imagine is possible. (The brain doesn't allow flights of fantasy in this situation unless you're *absolutely* sure that you're going to die).

CrossFire Guideline #72

*Use all of your abilities,
including your hidden ones,
and you can't help
but be amazing.*

Eyes on the Tiger

Many years ago on a clear hot day I found myself in the company of an attractive young lady showing me the local sights in a faraway place. We were strolling around the top of the mountain island of Penang, Malaysia. The con-

crete path had dense jungle on one side and cliffs dropping away to the ocean on the other.

As we walked, suddenly a deep, powerful roar assaulted us. I could literally feel the sound passing though me. Its owner had to be quite close.

Stopping and turning toward my companion, I whispered, somewhat incredulously, "Is that what I think it is?"

"Yes," she said quietly in her Australian accent, "it's a tiger."

"Should we be worried about this?" I asked.

"Not to worry," she answered nervously with a smile, "they rarely eat Yanks."

"Great!" I muttered and turned to resume our walk. Instantly, I was aware of rustling in the jungle ahead. I froze and signaled my friend to do likewise. We didn't have to long to wait.

After a few seconds, about twenty yards ahead of us and to the left, the jungle parted and a beautiful and very large Asian tiger stepped silently out onto the path. Turning toward us, his eyes immediately focused on us. He stared intensely. He was obviously considering whether to invite us to dinner.

Simultaneously we flashed into survival mode. Without removing our eyes from the tiger, we quickly examined all our options. Almost instantly and without saying a word, we both came to exactly the same conclusion.

*If attacked, the only real possibility for sur-
vival would be to dive over the cliff at the right
of us. It wasn't quite vertical and had many
large and sturdy bushes down its face. We were
confident that we could stop our descent before
slamming into the ocean far below. A water
landing wouldn't be pretty.*

*Trying any escape through the jungle or
along the path would be suicide. There we
stood. Frozen. Waiting for the tiger to make his
move.*

*Unbelievably, he must have decided that we
weren't really the kind of people he'd enjoy
dining on. (Maybe these tigers really didn't like
"Yanks.") Slowly he turned back toward the
jungle and leapt back in. We heard him quickly
receding into the distance.*

*Looking back on it, I'm not absolutely sure
that we would've survived our plan. Neverthe-
less, I am sure that we were as ready, willing,
and able to try as hard as any two humans on
the planet.*

*Besides, if he had pursued us, maybe we
would've gotten to see a real flying tiger!*

Your entire being is supercharged, with every
single part of you ready and anxious to do whatever it takes to survive. To help your brain
quickly decide the best course of action, your
senses are cranked up all the way. Each and every

one of them amplifying the effects of all the others.

Your vision now works like a telescope, your hearing like a huge antenna, your touch is electric, your balance is like a gyroscope, and you can smell things a bloodhound would miss. You even "know" the exact orientation and location of every part of your body to within one quarter of an inch.

CrossFire Guideline #73

You'll think your clearest and act your most decisive when you're in the greatest danger.

All these hyperactive sensors are connected to your brain that's now recording seconds as though they were hours. Every potentially useful memory zooms through your head (e.g., your life passing before your eyes). Every possible solution is analyzed, evaluated, and prioritized. The moment action is required, the best solution available will be executed with astonishing speed.

The net effect is that at that instant you have a clearer connection to the world around you than at almost any other time in your life. Living through the next few moments has got your full attention.

Now *that's* focus!

> ## CrossFire Guideline #74
>
> *The effort you expend on achieving any goal is directly proportional to its importance to you, personally.*

Magnifying Glass Effect

Learning to focus all your energy and concentration on a single goal, for even the briefest moment, can achieve spectacular results. We've all heard, and usually dismissed, stories of people using this fabulous hidden talent.

Power to the People

Some examples of the more physical aspects of this ability are:

- *A petite woman lifts a two-ton car off a trapped child.*

- *Someone tries a sport or game for the first time and plays like an expert.*

- *An ambushed soldier, hopelessly outnumbered and outgunned, not only survives but wins the battle.*

- *The ill-prepared student violinist who's only practiced a piece a few times and never gotten it right, does a solo in front of a large audience and nails it.*

- *A very old and tiny martial arts expert simultaneously humbling multiple younger, stronger, faster, and better skilled opponents with little effort.*

In addition to countless others. These are all situations where the person feels that they must absolutely succeed. Failure is seen as too dangerous, too deadly, too embarrassing, or too unthinkable to even contemplate.

When your mind makes that strong of a statement to itself, the rest of you will listen and do everything in its power to deliver the expected results.

Miracle Man

You can probably think of a few times that you even amazed yourself with your abilities. You're not alone. These events aren't fairy tales. These kinds of "miracles" happen all the time.

Not long ago each of us would've needed these "flashes" just to survive childhood.

This primal skill joins your mind, spirit, and body into a whole that is greater than the sum of the pieces. With it mankind has been elevated to the dominant species on this planet.

Together your mind and body are a remarkably efficient machine. Knowing that danger can appear suddenly, this wonderful tool stays prepared by remaining relaxed. Like the lions on the savannahs in Africa, it spends virtually its (your) entire life laying about. All but 5% of your brain lies dormant. Even for the athletic among us, 90% of our physical capacity is rarely used.

Very few of us even understand what we're capable of. Staggering. The loss to the world is unimaginable.

Each of us already has this gift. It's buried in our unconscious mind. The trick is to develop the skills and discipline necessary to bring it to the surface when we need it. With it you can then use this natural ability to take your strengths and abilities to spectacular levels.

Spying Your Future

Seeing the future requires more than just curiosity. It takes something special like creating your own Futurescope (the enchanted telescope we discussed way back on page 14). Building one of these isn't that hard. Like all telescopes, it's just a tube with the proper lenses in it. The only thing special is what the lenses are made of.

Your Own Magic

Looking inside one of these telescopes, you'd find three unique lenses. Together they allow you to bring your future into sharp focus. They are: your personal code of conduct, your understanding of the limitations and problems of leadership, and your ability to neutralize the obstacles that get in your way.

Your personal armor and shields make up a passive lens that has several unique benefits. It will help deflect troublesome detractions before you even notice them. This frees you from wasting your precious time and attention. It will minimize dangerous mind games by both you and the people you deal with. Your stress level will drop considerably overall and you'll minimize the chances of someone trying to stab you in the back. Finally, it will get most of the people that you come in contact with to help you along your way. This tremendously increases the odds of your success.

Obstacle handling is an active lens. It allows you to quickly categorize the problems in your path into types and apply the best technique to deal with each of them. This will save you even more time and effort. It also eliminates the stress usually associated with being unsure of how to handle them.

The last lens, the one in the middle—your understanding of leadership issues—mixes the passive and active aspects of the other two. It helps point you toward your goals, while removing the distortions caused by poor leadership. This prevents you from chasing your goals down useless dead ends.

CrossFire Guideline #75

True integrity with its sharp focus requires a high standard of personal conduct, understanding leadership's limitations, and the skills to neutralize obstacles.

Focus by the Numbers

Each of these three lenses represents a separate aspect of focus interrelated with the others. Think of them as multipliers:

√ Using all facets of your focus will give you outstanding results (10 x 10 x 10=1000).

√ Mediocre efforts overall will give you disappointing results (5 x 5 x 5=125).

√ Ignoring a single aspect altogether even with an otherwise impressive effort, will have disastrous effects (10 x 10 x 0=0).

√ Even small improvements in a single area can yield large gains overall (5 x 5 x 5 = 125 versus 6 x 5 x 5 = 150—a 20% gain!).

CrossFire Guideline #76

Small gains in one aspect of your integrity can yield large returns, but inattention to the same can doom you to failure.

With this versatile telescope in your hands, just a little fine adjustment on your part will help you find the best way home.

Sail on. ♦

Preview

Beyond limits
High expectations
Building momentum
Confidence
No waiting zone
Pot of gold

Online Supplement

www.IntegritysImpact.com/Action

Chapter 8

Ready to Go

"Great things are not done by impulse, but by a series of small things brought together."

—George Eliot

THROUGHOUT this book, we've covered many techniques, tips, and tricks to allow you to transform your dreams into reality. They all revolve around you achieving three simple and specific goals. Be more. Expect more. Achieve more. Right now!

Be More

Don't accept the status quo, especially for yourself. You can be so much more than you even now realize.

In military special forces training, candidates are pushed beyond their limits. This isn't done to break their spirit. Instead, it's meant to physically, emotionally, and mentally prove to each of them just how very much more they can become.

Often they find that they can endure three, five, even ten times more than they ever dreamed possible. That's an amazing amount of capacity that's goes unrecognized. But it's an even more amazing demonstration of everyone's potential.

Be more. Be much, much more. You have the ability inside you. Use it.

CrossFire Guideline #77

Always be more than anyone,
even you, expects.

Expect More

Once you start down the path of being more, it's natural to start expecting more from yourself and others. Don't fight it. You're helping yourself and others with your changes.

Low expectations do billions of dollars of damage to individuals as well as corporations. Contributing to the problem isn't the answer.

By expecting more from those around you, you're in effect saying that you believe in them. Don't take that away. Instead, tell them directly why your expectations are so high. Help them succeed.

As with anything, your goals for the people around you should be achievable. Placing too high an initial standard invites frustration for both of you. Keep it reasonable, yet not *too* reasonable.

With this approach you'll occasionally be disappointed. That's okay. The times that you aren't will more than make up for them.

CrossFire Guideline #78

Expect more to get more.

Achieve More

As you become more and you expect more, you can't help but achieve more. Don't stop when you do. You're on a roll. You'll find it much easier to attack the next goal with success fresh in your mind. Save the gloating until after you're dead.

The apparent ease of winning more battles after you've already won a few isn't imaginary. It's true. This is due to two factors. One is that you're becoming better at what you do. No surprise there.

The second is the less visible effect of confidence. It'll permeate your attitude. You may be unaware of it, but others won't be.

Over the years I've learned that in marginal situations, your confidence will often be the deciding factor between success and failure. It's a powerful ally. Don't leave home without it.

CrossFire Guideline #79

*Confidence is often
the only difference
between winning and losing.*

Right Now!

You picked up this book because you wanted to change for the better. You've now read it so you know that you've got the tools that you need. All you've got to do is start using them.

Not next month. Not next week. Not tomorrow. Right now! At this very moment start using what you've learned.

Adapt it, modify it, personalize it. Just start *using* it. Nothing will change until you do.

Sometimes you might find the first couple of weeks more difficult than you expected. This can be especially true if you've made massive changes in your personal conduct.

Some of the people around you may wonder out loud if you've grown too "good" for them. Ignore them. People are often critical of others trying to improve themselves.

CrossFire Guideline #80

Your time is your most precious asset. Spend it only on what's most important to you. Always.

After a few weeks you're going to start seeing some of the positive effects of your efforts. Intimate personal relationships will often improve first. Then friends and coworkers. Soon your boss(es) and subordinates will begin to notice.

Keep it up. It only gets better from here. Winning will start to come more often. You'll find yourself happier and more relaxed. Eventually, even the size of your bank account will start to swell.

Life is good. Bank on it. ♦

Preview

About the author
Education and training
Clients and companies
Valuable people

Online Supplement

www.IntegritysImpact.com/Credits

Appendix A

Key Points of Light

THIS book is the first of a series covering the many facets of the CrossFire method. This comprehensive and on-target approach to solving business problems didn't just appear one day out of the mist. Instead, it has come into focus over the last twenty years with the help of many people and organizations.

With such tremendous support, it's only fitting to take a few moments to thank some of these key points of light.

Author's Brief

Before doing that though, I should probably give you a little background on myself. After college, the U.S. Navy, and a few years of working as an employee for a couple of high technology companies, I went rogue and became an entrepreneur.

Since then, I've started around eleven business-to-business service companies, the most successful of which were/are CompuSolve, Jobline, Budget Payroll Services, and Uncommon Technology. The most recent one, Uncommon, has been around since 1994 and specializes in helping businesses solve their complex business problems.

Other than writing a few articles for magazines, a number of user manuals, and *way* too many project documents, this is my first book. In the media I've been interviewed by KCBS radio (SF, CA), BBB TV (San Jose, CA), *Infoworld, Portland Tribune* (OR), *Peninsula Times-Tribune* (SF, CA), and others regarding the innovations developed by my companies.

When not working, I generally split my spare time between family, my '70s musclecars (Road Runners, GTXs, Street Kitcar), my 1966 34' Fairliner boat (the fastest hunk of junk on the Columbia River), or scaring myself silly being adventurous. I like hiking, mountain climbing, skiing (both types), boating, scuba diving, driving too fast, fishing, martial arts, reading, movies, RTS computer games, gadgets, and much more. Argh! I'm so confused. I can't figure out if I'm a geek, a nerd, a jock, a tree hugger, a grease monkey, or a couch potato.

My wife Barbara, our three children, and I live near Portland, Oregon.

That's more than enough about me, on to the important people . . .

Schools and Training

Four schools were very important to the development of CrossFire and my own personal skills: St. Mary's College, U.C. Berkeley, Stanford University, and the U.S. Navy.

St. Mary's College, in Moraga, California developed and distributed the St. Mary's Math Quiz when I was in high school. This wicked list of ten open-ended questions was so hard that it could take weeks of work to get just one right answer. Because it encouraged creative solutions over stock answers, it sparked my unique approach to solving complex problems.

The University of California at Berkeley and its Lawrence Hall of Science allowed kids like me in the late 1960's to spend countless hours using the university's computers though we weren't even students.

When I was older, the engineering school at Berkeley enrolled me as a student when my grades weren't good enough, but my test scores were. After a year of taking *way* too many units while working full-time, the Dean understood when I bailed out (though he couldn't figure out how I had survived for so long).

They even accepted me back when I returned with my G.I. Bill scholarship and then reluctantly agreed with my reasoning when I immediately turned around and went to work in the rapidly emerging computer industry.

Stanford University's libraries with their open access were indispensable to me. When developing my first commercially successful software product, I needed a nearly impossible solution to a problem. I wanted to develop an indexing scheme for databases that was faster than anything else available. Using some inventiveness of my own coupled with ideas gleaned from hundreds of research papers, a solution emerged. Successfully coming up with that ultra-fast indexing method is probably the earliest use of what later became the CrossFire method.

My time in the U.S. Navy taught me about training, dealing with people, structure, perseverance, competition, self-sacrifice, politics, and security. It was an intense, gratifying, and frightening experience. I've never forgotten for even a moment the lessons I learned there. Luckily for me, the experience was just unpleasant enough that I didn't reenlist.

Organizations and Clients

Very important to CrossFire was the work of the Jet Propulsion Laboratory (JPL) on its MBASIC and Deep Space Network (DSN) development projects. Their desire to create 90% solutions in 10% of the time was a radical departure from NASA's "let's check it over and over again" approach. It's these projects and the techniques they used that helped define much of CrossFire's rapid, team-oriented development method.

The first company I worked for professionally was Basic Timesharing (the fourth computer company listed in Silicon Valley's yellow pages at the time . . . Abacus, Able, Ball, *Basic*). After hiring me, they tried a one-off experiment of having me work in every manufacturing group for about three months each. When finished, I had worked on everything the company made. Over the following years, I went from Systems Integration, to Software Development, to Marketing. Overall, I ended up with an intense, three and a half year course on all facets of running a successful computer company.

My former and current clients gave the Cross-Fire method its trial by fire and final tempering. Their comments, criticisms, and praise helped give CrossFire its versatility and strength. In particular, I'd like to thank those people I've worked with at Informix, AT&T, Cisco Systems, Zacson, Silicon Valley Bank, and Delta Dental for their high praise of CrossFire. They also strongly encouraged me to "get off my tail" and write the book, so that they could use CrossFire all by themselves.

The first successful company I started was CompuSolve, a business semi-custom software and service company. Our second client was Penvalve, owned at the time by Bruce Black. His faith in me and my company helped me to better understand entrepreneurs and their strong need to succeed. Constantly driving my team and myself toward excellence, he gave us a break when we really need it.

Very Important People

As one of the members of my former Board of Directors of CompuSolve, Mike DeSantis, one of the founders of Applied Process Technology (CompuSolve's very first client), always had an idea or opinion ready to help. His constant question at each Board meeting of "Is it time to sell yet?" always kept me focused on what was really important.

Mary Hale, CFO of Taos Mountain, and Samba Murthy, cofounder of XaQti, have my special appreciation for pounding me over the head with "Write the book!" Their convincing arguments that most organizations needed the CrossFire method got me started writing. Their strong faith in CrossFire and me helped me to finally finish it.

Lifelong friends from boyhood: David Williams, Scott Sorensen, Peter Shyvers, and Michael Dreese have been my comrades from childhood, through Berkeley (except for Mike, the heretic, who went to M.I.T.), to business, and life beyond. We have shared adventures, mountains, cars, crises, experiences, conflicts, secrets, joys, and sorrows. They're my irreplaceable cabinet of top advisors and companions through life.

My wife, Barbara, is a lifelong friend and intimate who has put up with me for thirty years. She's worked for me, and I've worked for her. She's put up with my uncontrollable urge to create: new companies, new products, new ideas, new everything. She's watched and supported me, always with a realistic eye, as I've gambled our futures. Demonstrating the power of faith, she's always been there for me.

Thanks to all of you. You've made life fun and this book possible.♦

Preview

CrossFire method defined
Reasons for multiple books
Troubleshooter series explained
Personal and professional benefits
Business problems addressed
A better way

Online Supplement

www.IntegritysImpact.com/CrossFire

Appendix B

About CrossFire

I 'VE spent the last 25 years helping very small to very large organizations solve their difficult business problems. In that time, I've seen the same mistakes repeated over and over and over again. Mistakes that could've easily been prevented by a little candid advice and a nudge or two in the right direction at the right time.

Out of those experiences, I created a technique for solving business problems that anyone with a few simple tools and a knowledge of the process can use. Its name is the CrossFire method. It's a very flexible framework for quickly dealing with all kinds of business issues. Its practical, step-by-step approach makes it easy for you to use, yet hard to make mistakes with. It's an excellent tool for anyone seriously looking for success.

CrossFire: A Definition

In a nutshell, CrossFire gives you the ability to gather critical information, identify key issues, determine the real needs, resolve conflicts, design a workable and unanimously supported solution, construct or acquire the new processes required, and successfully deploy them where needed. Whew! What a mouthful.

Now doing all that work may sound staggering, but once you know how and if a situation demands it, the entire process can often be compressed into as little as a few hours!

Purpose of Multiple Books

Unfortunately, the fine details of such a powerful technique can't be explained in a reasonably-sized book. Like learning to fly a modern jet fighter, it's best to break the process down into manageable chunks. In that spirit, I'm doing the same with the CrossFire method. This has the added advantage of allowing you to pick and choose those topics that meet your most immediate needs.

Troubleshooter's Arsenal

The first series of books is called *Trouble-shooter's Arsenal*. It covers all of the basic skills that the CrossFire method requires for its proper use. Now I naturally think they work best overall when coupled with the CrossFire method, but the truth is that these enhanced skills are extremely valuable no matter what approach to problems you may take.

In more detail this series examines the fundamentals of troubleshooting and solving business problems. It deals with the personal aspects of the job: developing sharp focus, effective leadership, eliminating distractions and obstacles, motivating and directing groups and teams to a common goal, working with (or around) individuals determined to address their own personal needs and agendas, staying organized, documenting and tracking information, picking the right problem-solving approach, and much much more.

These extremely important skills are often overlooked, taken for granted, or misunderstood. In the end they determine who you are, the rules you play by, your ability to work with individuals and groups, your understanding of corporate culture, and many aspects of your professional personality.

What happens inside your head and how well you work with others will not only dictate how well you solve problems, but how well you do in life. Make the effort to improve yourself and your skills. You won't regret it.

Answers for Hard Questions

Know you've got a business problem, but you can't quite put your finger on exactly what it is? Need to understand a difficult set of business issues, but it seems the more you learn the more confusing it becomes? Have a business headache that just won't go away, no matter what you throw at it?

Maybe you've got simple questions, but are getting useless answers. Do you need to know if a company is financially sound? Why a department is constantly behind? Who's really in control? Why everyone on the production line is so unhappy? How customers can be made more loyal? Where your competitor is going to strike next? How to survive an impending financial melt-down? Hard questions, every one of them. But if your organization didn't have problems they wouldn't need you, right? So how do you find the answers? Start by reading this book.

The CrossFire method was developed for any-one wanting a better understanding of what is really going on around them. Whether you've got problems to solve or issues to deal with, you'll benefit from the skills and techniques we cover.

Glimpsing the CrossFire

Whether you're straight out of school or you've been fending off business problems all your life, the CrossFire method gives you the tools and information needed to identify a huge range of business problems simply, quickly, and accurately. It's the easiest, fastest, and most cost-effective way to discover, analyze, and solve your important business problems.

The *Troubleshooter's* series of books is written for anyone wanting to take advantage of the benefits that this new approach offers. When used correctly, it'll help your company become more competitive, your department more effective and efficient, and you and your people more successful.

CrossFire and this book are directed at businesses and their problems, but it techniques don't have to be limited to that use only. Any person or organization that needs to solve simple to highly complex problems can benefit from its approach. This specifically includes individuals, government agencies, branches of the military, charitable organizations, and many others.

Matchmaking

We all have different needs. Something in the following list is meant to target yours. Scanning down the list, you'll see a variety of jobs and titles. Read any that may apply to you, skipping over the rest. (Reading the entire list might become somewhat tedious.)

For those of you who wear many hats, you'll probably find more than one that applies. That's okay. Regardless of the number, the ones you read cover the particular benefits of CrossFire for someone in your position.

- **CEO/CFO/COO/CIO/CTO/Business Owners.** Being responsible for an organization is an extremely demanding position. You need all the help you can get. The CrossFire method can be used to arm you or your own in-house calvary. With it you can get fast answers to tough questions without the endless delays and high costs of using outside resources. Even if you do decide to use outsiders, it'll help make sure that they're representing your best interests—not theirs.

- **Department/Group Managers.** Whether in business, government, the military, or charities any manager wants a smooth running operation. The CrossFire method can help you by minimizing your dependence on other groups. With it your department can diagnose and fix many of its own problems. CrossFire's precision targeting avoids wasting your current resources and helps you succeed where others fail.

• **IS/IT Managers and Supervisors.** System support is the biggest part of your job and your budget. Facing the customer's expectation that "all things are possible" is difficult at the very least. Using the CrossFire method can eliminate waste by focusing your limited resources where they'll do the most good. You'll be less reliant on consultants and contractors. When you address problems, you'll know that they'll get fixed right the first time.

• **Systems/Business Analysts.** You've spent a lot of time learning your trade and probably have a favorite method like Chin, Martin, Booch, Yourdon or something else for describing problems. Using the CrossFire method doesn't change that. CrossFire's primary focus is on the people portion of problems. Using it will make it much easier for you to succeed. It'll allow you to find the *real* issues and solutions quickly without having to constantly worry about dealing with inaccurate data or missing critical details.

• **IS/IT/Business Students.** The strongest element of your resume is how it demonstrates your capacity to solve an employer's problems. Learning the CrossFire method won't give you just another sentence to put on your resume. It'll give you a tremendous advantage over other untrained graduates and an equal or even greater advantage over the vast majority of people *already working your field!*

- **Programmers/Analysts.** Getting strong benefits from using the CrossFire method isn't difficult or elaborate. It's very flexible. Working with users on a regular basis, you've no doubt found that many of the solutions that they demand don't actually solve their problems. This is where CrossFire can help. With it you and they will zero in on the real issues and ensure that the solutions built will actually fix their problems.

- **Business/Management Consultants.** Tired of losing lucrative contracts to "Big Six" accounting/consulting firms because "They have a method in place for solving problems like ours."? It doesn't have to be that way. Learning the CrossFire method will give you the *best* approach to solving your client's complex business problems. It's designed to get accurate, practical answers quicker than any of the big guy's methods. Using Cross-Fire levels the playing field.

- **IS/IT/Business Instructors and Teachers.**
  Now you can give your students and yourself
  a reliable step-by-step method for address-
  ing difficult business problems. With it your
  students will be better prepared for the *real*
  business world than any of those that have
  gone before. Teaching the CrossFire method
  to your students will enhance and increase
  the value of *all* the other skills that you give
  them.

- **CPAs/Accountants/Financial Advisors.**
  You've spent a lot of time helping your small
  clients. Isn't it infuriating to lose those same
  long-term clients to bigger firms when they
  grow? Now you *can* fight back. Using the
  CrossFire method, you can preemptively
  attack your client's business problems
  before they start looking for "other" solutions. It'll give you a complete suite of
  top-notch techniques to develop accurate,
  practical answers quicker than any of your
  competitors.

- **Entrepreneurs/Venture Capitalists/Finan-
  cial Backers.** Starting and running a successful business requires money, knowledge, skill, and luck. Luck's impact can be a
  killer. Using the CrossFire method can minimize Lady Luck's negative impacts by really
  pumping up the knowledge and skills por-

tion of the formula. Use CrossFire to evaluate the marketplace, build internal systems, limit risks, develop contingency plans, and deal with an uncertain business climate.

- **Professionals/Executives.** Eighty percent of what you bring to a job are your problem-solving skills, not the knowledge of your field. Employers and clients are looking for people that can solve their particular problems. Using the CrossFire method will give you that ability and more. It'll provide you with a powerful array of new skills for dealing with issues, people, and change. No matter what problems may come at you next, you'll be well armed to deal with them.

- **Users of Broken Business Systems.** You need to get a job done and things just don't work right. Day after day you deal with the same problems. Requests for help go unread, complaints are ignored. What do you do? Use CrossFire. It'll help you discover the true extent of the problem, how much it's costing the organization, and what it'll take to fix it. Armed with CrossFire's clear description and justification of your needs, you can get your problems dealt with—now!

• **Anyone needing to solve problems and deal with people.** In this fast paced world of increasing isolation and faceless communications, people are losing the skills necessary to communicate effectively with others. Schools try, but don't give more than the basics for dealing with problems, at least where humans are involved. The CrossFire method does more. Use the skills it teaches to listen effectively to others, resolve misunderstandings, deal with politics, handle issues, attack problems aggressively, and develop practical solutions to all those roadblocks that'll come up in life.

Problems Under Attack

Fixing problems, both the known and the virtually invisible, is what CrossFire was designed for. Here's a sampling of the more common problems that it can help you solve. (Again, just skip over any that don't apply.)

• **Rapid Growth.** You've got a great product and the customers are just eating it up. If you're not careful, they'll eat the entire organization. Dealing with rapid growth is like running while shooting a gun—you're aim tends to be really awful. Using CrossFire will add a stabilizer to your sights. Even in the rush, you'll be able to see clearly and hit what you're aiming at. Now you'll be able to maximize the situation instead of just coping with it.

• **Legacy Systems.** Got a process, computerized or not, that's older than the wind? The procedures it uses are probably so tied up in tradition and habit that no one can even consider any other way of doing things. You know that there's got to be a better way. The CrossFire method will help you get past all the bad habits and find the company's real needs. With a fresh look, you'll be able to nail down what it takes to get the job done right in today's world—not yesterday's.

• **Emergencies**. The sky has fallen, so what do you do? Whether you've just found out about a lawsuit, investigation, sabotage, terrorism, tampering, power struggle, proxy fight, takeover, or something equally grave, you need information and a course of action—fast. How you handle the next day or even the next few hours can be critical. In hyper-accelerated situations CrossFire can give you critical direction and information in as little as a few hours. Other methods collapse under that kind of pressure.

• **Mission Changes.** Suddenly the market-place changes and you're expected to compensate. What do you do? Use CrossFire. It'll help you decide what can be salvaged and what has to change. Slicing through all the entrenched policies and procedures, it will lead you to a new comprehensive package that meets those requirements. Just because the world is now spinning upside down doesn't mean you have to stand on your head.

• **Key Processes.** Is there some system that is so critical to the organization's needs that every time it stutters, hesitates, or fails the management staff has a collective heart attack? Everyone knows it's got problems, but the idea of attempting to fix it and failing is a show stopper. Using the CrossFire method will let you safely navigate the minefield. You'll discover all the issues involved and how to accurately gauge the changes required. Go ahead and install that super-charger in the process that you always wanted.

• **Downsizing.** For a long time you've pushed your people to the very limit of their capacity. Now you're expected to continue with many of them missing. How's it even possible? By using CrossFire. Instead of letting work go undone, CrossFire will help you streamline the operation. Unnecessary, redundant, or marginal tasks can be eliminated. Your limited resources are free to concentrate on what's important. All of which can be implemented in a reasonably short period of time.

- **Mergers.** Everything's finally going smoothly and now you're expected to integrate your systems with another company that you've bought or has bought you. Headache city. Not necessarily. CrossFire can help you figure out what's really needed to fully integrate the two organizations without causing a disaster. It'll take the best of both approaches and integrate them into an even more powerful solution. One plus one can equal three, instead of just two.

- **Core Applications.** Do you have one central process or type of data that seems to touch every part of the organization? Even when it doesn't work right, it's such a monster, with tentacles touching everything, that even thinking of making changes can be frightening. CrossFire can help you tame the beast. With fear banished and the right tools in hand, you're free to tweak or reform the core to match the organization's current and future needs. Even tiny changes can have a profound effect on how well the company performs its job.

- **Shutdowns.** Too much capacity or too little demand and you'll find yourself faced with a plant shutdown. Whether its part of the business or all of it, CrossFire can help you minimize the loss and damage. Concentrating on where the value is, it'll show you what to sell off in pieces and what can go intact. It's an ugly situation, but successfully handling it can help the organization, its people, its creditors, and you.

- **Unionization.** In many industries unions may or may not be a part of business. Regardless of whether a union is potentially coming in or has already arrived, you'll need to play by the rules. This isn't the time to bury your head in the sand. CrossFire can help you deal with the situation. Its organization and information gathering capabilities will assist you in structuring the best strategy and tactics possible. You'll need them to maximize any possible solutions.

- **New Functions.** Life doesn't stand still and either does your company. When you discover a hole in your product mix or internal processes, you'll need to fill it. Unlike fixing something that already exists, there's no framework to lift ideas from. You've got a clean slate. Let CrossFire help you fill it in right. Its structure will guide you through the creation process and help you build something that works well from scratch. First generation systems don't have to be a disaster.

- **Exploration.** Not all changes are "have tos." Sometimes you'll want to look at new things because you believe that they have potential. Exactly what that potential is, may still be a mystery. CrossFire can help you probe and poke until you find out exactly what its potential is. Maybe it's gold, maybe it's not, but CrossFire's method will show you where to look and what to examine. If there's gold around, you'll find it.

Last Word

Simply put, the CrossFire method is an easy to use, comprehensive, flexible, and reasonable approach for quickly solving a wide range of business problems. Regardless of whether the situation is complex or simple, CrossFire can provide you with a better understanding of the issues involved and the alternatives available.

All you have to do is use it. ♦

Preview

Story time
Fast and easy reading
Understanding and simplicity
Finding what you want
Changing things for the better

Online Supplement

www.IntegritysImpact.com/Features

Troubleshooter's Arsenal 1

Appendix C

Book Features

A lot of effort went into making this book faster to read and easier to understand than most others you've read. If we've done it right, you should be able to start using what you've learned almost immediately.

Most of the changes to this book's format are intuitive in nature and require little or no knowledge of their existence to take advantage of them. They're listed here for those people that want to get the absolute maximum out of this book or are just curious about how this book's format is different than others.

Aesop's Tales

Scattered throughout this book are a number of real life stories and example situations meant to illustrate key points or concepts. They can be identified by their italicized text. Their content may be serious, amusing, or curious. They're meant to help make it easier for you to remember important ideas or techniques.

When working with others, you're encouraged to use these or similar stories to help them understand your ideas. They're especially useful when trying to explain a difficult or complex concept.

Telling tales isn't a bad way to communicate. Most people like hearing stories from real life. Besides, you can always use them to break the ice when meeting new people.

If you're in a real rush, you can safely skip over them without missing any of CrossFire's key concepts. The only question is, without them will you still clearly remember those concepts later?

Reading Speed and Comfort

- Large, easy on the eyes, easy to comprehend type fonts for faster reading with less effort.

- The paper used has low reflectivity and very little show through for ease of reading under harsh lights. It's acid-free for a very long shelf life.

- The book's standard size (half a standard letter sheet and modest thickness) is convenient to carry, store and handle.

Clarity and Comprehension

- The words and sentences used are easy to understand. A college or even high school vocabulary isn't required to comprehend what's being said. It's also designed to be less difficult for those who use American English as a second language.

- The text is written in an informal, familiar style. Formality tends puts up barriers, barriers that CrossFire works hard to remove. The familiar style is designed to help you imagine that I'm talking to you directly, *because I am!*

- Each chapter and appendix is broken up into small and distinct sections and subsections. This allows you to read brief chunks and still benefit from cohesive ideas and concepts. All without requiring you to reread large sections just to "get it."

- Plenty of examples and samples are intermixed with the text to make learning faster, easier, and more enjoyable.

- Many real life stories are used to illustrate key concepts that are being discussed in the text. They're even referenced with italicized titles in "Contents" for easy access.

- For simplicity's sake, the male forms of words are used for reference and examples (e.g., he, him, man, etc.). This is not meant as a slight to females. It's simply that in English "one," "it," or mixing the use of he/she, his/her, etc. is tedious at best and unreadable at worst. Please forgive me.

- Overly technical terms and buzzwords are avoided to make the concepts easier to learn and more universal in appeal.

- Key concepts are pulled out and highlighted. Titled "CrossFire Guideline," they have ruled lines vertically on either side of the text. The number allows easy reference across all books covering the CrossFire method (the *Troubleshooter's* series) when referring to that particular concept.

- All extraneous or indirectly useful information is bundled in the appendices at the end of this book or in the online supplements. This is material that should assist you in using or better understanding the main body of the book, but it isn't absolutely required. It's there if you want or need it.

- Every chapter contains a brief summary at the end. This restates the key concepts covered. If it doesn't match what you've learned, then you need to read the chapter again more carefully.

Navigation and Reference

- Uncluttered, consistent page numbers are located on the lower outside edge of all pages except for the first three (that are title pages) and the last (which is an order form). Pages are numbered consecutively with clear, simple Arabic numbers. No Roman numerals. No confusing "Chapter-Page" formats. This format allows faster look ups.

- "Contents" at the front of the book provides a quick reference by title of this entire book. This allows you to do fast chapter, section, subsection, and story specific look ups. It starts on the left-hand page to minimize page flipping when searching it.

- Chapters always start on a right-hand page and have large numbers with somewhat smaller titles. That first page and the one directly to its left have no header (the section or chapter title information listed on top of most pages) so that you can quickly find the start of a chapter by flipping pages.

• A summary of each chapter and appendix is located across from its title on the left-hand page. It's labeled "Preview" in bold text. It contains brief descriptions of the topics covered in the order that they appear.

• A special web address is located on chapter and appendix "Preview" pages. It's at the bottom of the page under the bold "Online Supplement." This is your key to additional information and resources online.

• The top left-hand page in each chapter and appendix show its number/letter and name. The right-hand page shows the section name. This makes it easier to find a particular section of the book.

• A "♦" is used to mark the end of a chapter or appendix, so that you can skip forward to the next one (by turning the page).

• A detailed index in the back of this book allows you to look up specific information quickly. For topics covered in multiple locations, the primary location will be italicized.

- "See also" in the index is rarely used.

- The top of each index page shows the range of topics on that page just like in a dictionary. This makes finding words or phrases easier.

Allowances for Customizing

- Generous page margins for you to make notes or comments next to the text.

- Reasonable amounts of white space in and around the text so that you can highlight passages and insert comments.

- An occasional page is located at the end of a chapter for you to record more detailed comments or notes. It's labeled "Reader's Notes" at the very top of the page.

Point of the Exercise

All of these various changes and enhancements are designed to make this book as easy to understand and use as possible. If you think I'm wrong or you've got a suggestion, I'd appreciate hearing from you (see *Contact Info* on page 209). ♦

Preview

Our (your) contribution
Why pick hepatitis?
What's the money used for?

Online Supplement

www.IntegritysImpact.com/Hepatitis

Appendix D

Helping Those in Need

"We stand at the precipice of a grave threat to our public health . . . It affects people from all walks of life, in every state, in every country. And unless we do something about it soon, it will kill more people than AIDS."

—C. Everett Koop

BOTH true integrity and the CrossFire method are powerful weapons for conquering many of society's ills, but they aren't all powerful. There are many other tools that can be used to address our community's needs. Charity is one tool that's both unique and powerful.

Leading by Example

Uncommon Technology and I believe that charity is both a corporate and an individual responsibility. To come up with a sound and reasonable plan to fulfill that need, we examined what other organizations are doing. From a corporate standpoint the overall results were, for lack of a better word, disappointing.

By virtue of being a small publisher, Uncommon Technology has more flexibility in our business practices than many of our competitors. Because of this and our beliefs we've made a typically "uncommon" if not unique decision regarding corporate giving.

We will give to the selected charity ten percent (10%) of UTI's net profit from the sale of each and every copy of Integrity's Impact! For those people that receive a free or promotional copy of this book, we ask that you give $5 to the charity of your choice.

Perceived Need

"It is suspected that there are, at present, more than 5 million people in the United States that are infected with Hepatitis C [HCV], and perhaps as many as 200 million around the world. This makes it one of the greatest public health threats faced in this century . . ."

"Without rapid intervention to contain the spread of the disease, the death rate from hepatitis C will surpass that from AIDS . . . and [it] will only get worse."

Quoted from the *www.epidemic.org* web site sponsored by the Trustees of Dartmouth College.

One of the most insidious aspects of this epidemic is that *most of the people infected don't even know that they have it!* In many people the disease doesn't reveal itself with symptoms for ten or more years. By the time they find out, it could already be too late to save them.

Being frank, I have a very strong personal interest in HCV. My wife contracted it in 1985 from tainted blood she receive during ankle surgery for a horseback riding accident. Since then the disease has destroyed her liver and nearly killed her several times. She's currently awaiting a liver transplant. A cure probably won't help her, but it *would* save millions of others.

Charity's Focus

These funds will be used to support finding a cure for hepatitis C. For the name of the currently selected charity, links on hepatitis, UTI's charitable contributions, or other related matters, please visit the web address listed under *Online Supplement* back on page 204.

Thank you for helping us to support them. ♦

Your Ideas Matter

U NLIKE most other methods for solving problems, CrossFire evolves. It changes as the times and situations warrant. When the pace of business quickens, so does Cross-Fire's speed and accuracy in providing answers. Its superior strength lies in its ability to adapt. New ideas are what keeps it fresh. Ideas from people like you.

In the last two decades, the CrossFire method has been tested, refined, and improved in real situations and on important issues. (For more detailed information on CrossFire, please check out Appendix B starting on page 179.)

Because of everyone's effort, CrossFire has successfully solved many, many problems in all kinds of companies, the sizes of which range from one-man operations to huge multinational corporations.

Making a Difference

As a reader of this book, I need your help. You can improve CrossFire and future editions of

Integrity's Impact by sending me your stories, comments, corrections, suggestions, and ideas. Please let me know about any inaccuracies, confusing or misleading statements, or errors that you might find. Any examples or stories about your experiences with integrity would also be welcome. I will try to incorporate all reasonable suggestions into future editions.

Help CrossFire and *Integrity's Impact* continue to improve. Your experience and ideas are an important part of the process.

Contact Info

Please send your suggestions and ideas to:

Integrity's Impact—Ideas
Uncommon Technology Inc.
5400 Carillon Point
Kirkland WA 98033 USA

or email me at:

Ideas@IntegritysImpact.com

CrossFire has always been a team effort. You're now part of the team. I look forward to hearing from you. ♦

Index

M magnifying glass effect: 158-159
management consultants: 186
McKinley, William: 79
McMahon, Edward: 90
mergers: 192
messiness: 67-69
military special forces training: 166
mission changes: 191
mistakes, taking responsibility for:
    20, 34-35, 39, *49-50*
motivation, as a leadership skill: 128-129
Mount McKinley climbing trip example
    avoiding bears: 116-117
    delay of: 109-110
    ignoring car problem: 111-112
    integrating reality: 113-115
    quitting to survive: 121-122
    resolving problems: 118-119
Murthy, Samba: 176-177

N NASA: 175
navigation and reference: 201-203
naysayers: *76-79*, 169
networking: 65-66

O obstacle handling: *105-125*, 181
    avoiding: *115-117*, 123
    delaying: *109-110*, 123, 146-147
    ignoring: *110-112*, 123
    integrating: *112-115*, 124
    methods: 105

power in dangerous situations: 153-160
problems
    and CrossFire method: 189-194
    as part of job: 50
processes, key: 191
procrastination: 108
professionals: 188
programmer/analysts: 186
promises, keeping: 40-42
proximity, as power factor: 93-94
public speaking: 44

Q   quitting: *120-122*, 124

R   rapid growth: 189-190
reading speed and comfort: 198-199
real life stories and examples: 198
resolving obstacles: *117-119*, 124
responsibility for mistakes:
    20, *34-39*, 49-50
rubber example: 77-78

S   sandwich tracking example: 142-145
scandals: 19-21
secrets, keeping: 40-42
Shaw, George Bernard: 31
shields against distractions: *57-83*, 161
    compensating for biases: 62-64
    courtesy: 60-62
    independence: 75-82
    knowledge: 64-66

UNCOMMON TECHNOLOGY

Where reality is only a dream away.